To Mum

from Carol & Jimmy

With love — Christmas 2001.

EX LIBRIS

BOOK OF
JAMS, JELLIES AND CHUTNEYS

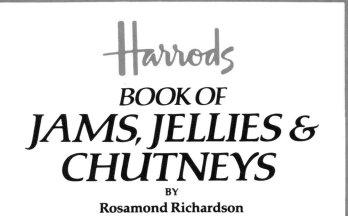

Harrods
BOOK OF
JAMS, JELLIES &
CHUTNEYS

BY
Rosamond Richardson

Grange
BOOKS

Published by Grange Books
An Imprint of Grange Books PLC
The Grange
Grange Yard
London SE1 3AG

This edition published 1994

ISBN 1 85627 584 1

First published by Ebury Press
Random House
20 Vauxhall Bridge Road
London SW1V 2SA

First Impression 1986

—————————◆—————————

EDITORS: Fiona MacIntyre and Barbara Croxford
ART DIRECTOR: Frank Phillips
DESIGNERS: Marshall Art
PHOTOGRAPHY: Grant Symon
STYLIST: Sue Russell
COOKERY: Susanna Tee, Janet Smith and Maxine Clark

Ebury Press would like to thank Harrods, and their archivist
Margaret Baber, for allowing the use of the black and white
illustrations taken from Harrods catalogues.

Computerset by MFK Typesetting Ltd, Hitchin, Herts
Printed and bound in Italy by New Interlitho Spa, Milan

Contents

HERE is nothing quite like the personal satisfaction which comes from producing a wide range of home-made preserves – not only the making of them, but also the glorious sight of a store cupboard full of jams, jellies and chutneys. The satisfaction comes partly from mastering a craft, partly from knowing that you are utilizing a harvest to its full and partly from the joy of putting good food by for future use when the ingredients are no longer in season. Sometimes there is the added satisfaction of bringing the countryside into the kitchen, particularly during the late summer and early autumn when the hedgerows and fields bear their annual harvest of berries, nuts and mushrooms. These foods, all free for the picking, introduce new and interesting tastes to the palate, and open up an exciting range of original combinations to experiment with. The principal delight of this is that the activity involved – a pleasant country ramble rather than an expedition to the supermarket – is pleasurable and relaxing. By hoarding the fruits of the countryside, it gives us a chance to enjoy the misty, slightly chill days of autumn as the sun sinks lower in the sky and winter draws on.

Your range of preserves can be as simple or as exotic as you choose: there is as much virtue in the simplest strawberry jam as in a mixed preserve using rare tropical fruits, or an unusual and delicately spiced chutney. For the adventurous cook who likes to experiment, however, the increasing availability of unusual fruits and vegetables makes for an exciting and creative challenge. Multicoloured fruit and vegetables flown in fresh from all over the world are stacked high in gleaming piles, making our markets and supermarkets more exciting places than ever.

So here is a new range of unusual as well as simple recipes, ranging through jams both ordinary and extraordinary, and classic as well as unconventional marmalades. There are unusual jellies to go with both hot and cold meals, delicate fruit curds and cheeses, oriental chutneys and relishes, and crisp, tangy pickles, both sweet and sour, as well as some luxurious speciality conserves. The recipes utilize traditional ingredients as well as unusual combinations of exotic produce, fruit that can be gathered from the wild, and fruit and vegetables that you can grow yourself. With the loving care and artistry that goes into the skill of successful preserving, a new look at experimenting with novel combinations of fruits and vegetables, herbs and spices, flowers and leaves, will develop a further intuition about mingling flavours and textures, as well as delighting the most demanding of palates.

Jams

MAKING jam is almost synonymous, for some people, with homeliness, and indeed there is something about the seasonal smells as it is cooking and about the neat rows of glistening jars on the larder shelf, that is both comforting and satisfying. Above all, though, the taste of home-made jam is quite incomparable with even the best brand names, and there are so many fruits to choose from nowadays that you can try out exciting new combinations that manufacturers have not yet thought of. Once the simple elements of jam-making have been mastered, it becomes a part of home-making which gives family and friends alike nostalgic memories through the years.

ESSENTIAL INGREDIENTS FOR
→ JAM-MAKING ←

Fruit
The fruit should be firm and ripe, or just under-ripe, and always fresh and of good quality. Never use over-ripe fruit because, since the pectin in it is changing to pectin acid, the jam will not set. In a wet season, fruit has a lower sugar content than normal so there is an increased tendency to mildew and therefore less chance of long-term sound keeping. Always wash or rinse fruit before use to remove any traces of dust or dirt, and to clean off any chemicals with which it may have been treated. Remember that the greengrocer is not your only source of fruit – fruits from the garden and fruits from the countryside enhance the sense of satisfaction that is such an integral part of jam-making.

Sugar

Use lump, preserving or granulated sugar – in that order of preference. You can also use raw cane sugar although this tends to crystallise more easily on storage. Avoid the dark sugars since they change the colour of the fruit and tend to spoil its flavour. Sugar is a vital factor in the setting process, and the necessary level is between 55% and 70%, although a high acid content in the fruit makes the exact sugar balance less critical. If you warm the sugar slightly before stirring into the fruit, it will dissolve more quickly.

If your jam should crystallise during storage, this is due to either too much sugar, or to over-boiling; it also results if the storage place is too dry. You can employ a short-term remedy by turning the contents of the jar into a saucepan and heating gently to near-boiling point. Re-pot in a warm, clean jar. The jam will be satisfactory for immediate use, however, it will go sugary again in time.

Pectin

Pectin is a natural, gum-like substance found in varying amounts in different fruits, usually in their cores, pips and skins. Its presence is essential to a good set in jams and jellies. Pectin content is particularly high in the pips and white pith of citrus fruits, and in sour apples. There are some fruits which do not contain enough pectin and acid to provide a good set, so the answer is either to mix low pectin fruits with high pectin ones, or to add commercial pectin which can be bought in liquid or powder form. It substantially reduces the cooking time so is a labour-saving device if not an entirely economical one.

GUIDE TO THE PECTIN CONTENT
→ OF FRUITS →

HIGH	MEDIUM	LOW
cooking apples	*fresh apricots*	*cherries*
blackcurrants	*early blackberries*	*elderberries*
cranberries	*greengages*	*figs*
damsons	*loganberries*	*medlars*
gooseberries	*peaches*	*mulberries*
lemons	*plums*	*pears*
grapefruit	*raspberries*	*rhubarb*
acid plums	*sweet apples*	*strawberries*
quinces		*late blackberries*
redcurrants		*marrow*
loganberries		*guavas*
grapes		

→ ACID →

Tartaric Acid

Tartaric acid is an organic acid common in plants, and found in especially high quantities in sour fruits. It is marketed in powdered form, and can be used to assist the setting of jams – to every 900 g (2 lb) fruit used, dissolve 5 ml (1 tsp) tartaric acid in a little water and add to the pan at the end of the cooking process.

Citric Acid

Citric acid is a fairly weak organic acid found in the juice of lemons and other citrus fruits. It is a souring agent and preservative, and is available commercially in crystalline form. Pure lemon juice is also a good setting agent – use 30 ml (2 tbsp) to every 900 g (2 lb) fruit.

EQUIPMENT FOR JAM MAKING

Preserving Pan

Choose a pan which will be large enough: it should not be more than half-full when the fruit and sugar are added, because it needs to be able to boil rapidly without boiling over. Choose a heavy-bottomed aluminium or stainless steel pan for best results – never use iron or zinc pans since the acid in the fruit will attack the metal and the colour and flavour of the jam will be destroyed. Enamel pans do not conduct heat fast enough for satisfactory jam-making and tend to burn easily; tin may melt! You can use a copper pan if you like, but be sure to remove all traces of polish before cooking the fruit, and be aware that much of the vitamin C content will be destroyed by its reaction with the metal.

➔ OTHER EQUIPMENT ◆

wooden spoons – long-handled for preference to ensure that they do not disappear beneath the simmering preserve. Metal spoons conduct heat too fast for comfortable handling and may be discoloured by the acid.

large hair or nylon sieve – a metal sieve will impair the flavour of the preserve and can also be discoloured by the acid in the fruit.

slotted spoon
sharp stainless steel knives for chopping and slicing the fruit
serrated knife
chopping board
juice squeezer
mincer with both fine and coarse blades AND/OR a **food processor**
stoner for stoning fruit
wide-lipped jug for pouring
funnel
jam thermometer
accurate scales
double boiler for some curds etc.
plastic screw–top jars
waxed and cellophane discs
labels

BEST STRAWBERRY JAM (page 15)

➤ BASIC METHOD ➤

A jam is a conserve of fruit boiled with sugar and water, whereas a jelly is the fruit juice only boiled with sugar, and a marmalade is a kind of jam made with citrus fruits. Jams must have sufficient sugar for sound storage – organisms cannot grow when the sugar content is over 50–55%. Hence the addition of lemon juice in many recipes – its twofold purpose being to relieve the sweetness and to help the set. Jams are usually cooked to 105°C (221°F).

Remember that it is the fruit rather than the sugar that needs cooking, so jams and jellies boiled for too long with the sugar tend to lose colour and flavour. Certainly soft fruits can be ruined by long boiling – they need just a short cooking time before the sugar is added.

To start with, smear a butter paper over the bottom and sides of a preserving pan before putting the fruit in – this will help prevent burning during the cooking process. An old country custom is to put a marble into the bottom of the pan for the same purpose (removing it before potting) – and it works!

Put the fruit into the pan, with or without water added as instructed in the recipe, and cook gently until the juices begin to run before bringing to boiling point. Simmer until the fruit is tender, then add the sugar – warmed for preference as it will dissolve more quickly. Stir over a gentle heat until the sugar has completely dissolved. Bring to the boil again and boil rapidly to setting point.

➤ TESTING FOR SET ➤

Flake Test
When the jam begins to thicken, dip in a wooden spoon and hold it over the pan. If, as the jam drops off the spoon, it forms a sheet and drops off as cleanly as a flake, then the jam will set when cold. If by any chance the jam fails to set, add 30 ml (2 tbsp) lemon juice per 1.8 kg (4 lb) fruit and try again – or add commercial pectin in the quantity suggested on the label.

Saucer Test
When the jam starts to thicken, put a teaspoonful of the mixture on to a cold saucer and put it in a cold place. Draw the pan of jam off the heat. Wait for 5 minutes, then tilt the saucer. If the jam wrinkles a little and does not run, it is ready for

potting. If it is still liquid and runs over the saucer, return the jam to the heat and continue boiling until the test is successful. Generally speaking, the stage of boiling the sugar to setting point takes about 10 minutes.

Thermometer

You will need a good cook's thermometer which goes up to and includes 104°C (220°F). Always put a thermometer into hot water before use to prevent it cracking. To test for set, stir the jam so that the temperature is even throughout, and when the thermometer reads 104°C (220°F) a good set should be obtained – although in some cases 105–6°C (221–222°F) will be better.

THE FINAL TOUCH

A knob of butter added just before the end of the cooking gives the jam a shine, and also makes scum easier to remove since it collects the scum in one place. Lift the scum off with a metal spoon and discard. If there are any more traces of scum, these are easily removed by dipping absorbent kitchen paper on to them and lifting off. Pure glycerine, stirred in 2–3 minutes before the jam is ready to pot, will increase its preserving qualities – use 5 ml (1 tsp) glycerine to every 1.8 kg (4 lb) jam. A good jam will be stiff without being solid, clear and not cloudy, and have a good flavour.

POTTING AND COVERING

Choose suitably sized jam jars with plastic screw-tops. Wash and rinse them thoroughly in hot water. Dry and then keep the jars warm in a very low oven until ready for use. Pour or ladle the jam into the jar until filled up to the neck. Cover immediately with a waxed disc, waxed-side down, to keep any dust out. Leave to cool, then place a cellophane disc over the top of the jar and screw the plastic top down over it. Avoid using metal screw-tops as they have a tendency to corrode and rust. Wipe the jars clean. Label clearly, with the date as well as the contents, and store.

STORAGE

Choose a cool, dark, dry place: heat will shrink the contents of the jar, light will fade the colour of the jam, and damp will encourage mould.

Raspberry and Rhubarb Jam

This delicious, summery jam is an unusual combination of two fruits which are often abundant at the same time. It is freshly sharp, a gorgeous pink colour and a superb jam on freshly baked scones.

900 g (2 lb) rhubarb
450 g (1 lb) raspberries
150 ml (¼ pint) water
1.4 kg (3 lb) sugar

MAKES 2.3 kg (5 lb)

Wash and cut the rhubarb into 2.5 cm (1 inch) lengths. Hull and rinse the raspberries.

Put the rhubarb into a preserving pan with the water. Cover and simmer for about 10 minutes until tender. Remove the lid and boil fast to reduce to a thick pulp.

Add the raspberries to the pan with the sugar. Stir over a low heat until the sugar has dissolved. Bring to the boil and boil rapidly for about 10 minutes, stirring occasionally, or until setting point is reached.

Skim the jam, pot in warm, clean jars and cover. Seal while still hot.

Gooseberry, Strawberry and Elderflower Jam

The exceptional and pungent flavour of elderflowers gives an exquisite taste to this mixture of two of our best summer fruits. Together they combine to make an extraordinarily tasty and fragrant jam.

700 g (1½ lb) gooseberries
700 g (1½ lb) strawberries
6 large elderflower heads

150 ml (¼ pint) water
1.4 kg (3 lb) sugar

MAKES 2.3 kg (5 lb)

Top, tail and wash the gooseberries. Hull and rinse the strawberries. Tie the elderflower heads in a muslin bag.

Put the gooseberries in a preserving pan with the water and bag of elderflowers. Simmer for about 15 minutes until the gooseberries are tender.

Add the strawberries to the pan and simmer for a further 3–4 minutes. Remove the bag of flowers and add the sugar. Stir over a low heat until the sugar has dissolved. Bring to the boil and boil rapidly for about 10 minutes, stirring occasionally, or until setting point is reached.

Skim the jam, pot in warm, clean jars and cover. Seal while still hot.

Summer Harvest Jam

This elegant jam is a celebration of the soft fruits of high summer. No matter which combination of berries you choose to use, the jam will be a lovely reminder of those sunny days.

1.8 kg (4 lb) mixed soft fruits, eg strawberries, raspberries, loganberries, redcurrants, blackcurrants, gooseberries, etc.

2.3 kg (5 lb) sugar

MAKES 3.6 kg (8 lb)

Hull and rinse the strawberries, raspberries and loganberries. Top, tail and wash the currants and gooseberries.

Put the fruit into a preserving pan with a little water – the amount will depend on the ripeness of the fruit – and simmer for 5 minutes.

Add the sugar and stir over a low heat until dissolved. Bring to the boil and boil rapidly for about 10 minutes, stirring occasionally, or until setting point is reached.

Pot the jam in warm, clean jars and cover. Seal immediately.

Best Strawberry Jam

Like most people, I like to make the most of the strawberry season while it is at its height. This jam, concocted under pressure of time one year, has become my family favourite and it honestly makes the best strawberry jam I have ever tasted. As with many of the low-pectin fruits, however, strawberry jam has a relatively short shelf-life, but that has never been a problem in my house – it vanishes all too quickly!

1.4 kg (3 lb) strawberries
900 g (2 lb) sugar
150 ml (¼ pint) water
thick slice of lemon

MAKES 1.4–1.8 kg (3–4 lb)

Hull and rinse the strawberries. Put into a preserving pan with the sugar, water and lemon slice. Simmer gently over a moderate heat until the sugar has dissolved. Bring to the boil and boil rapidly for about 10 minutes, stirring occasionally, or until setting point is reached.

Skim the jam, pot in warm, clean jars and cover. Seal while still hot.

Blackcurrant and Cherry Jam

This dark, rich, mouthwatering combination of fruits fully lives up to its description. It is inspired by an idea from the original edition of Mrs Beeton, who describes this jam as 'very delicious'.

900g (2 lb) blackcurrants	600 ml (1 pint) water
900 g (2 lb) black cherries	1.4 kg (3 lb) sugar

MAKES 2.3 kg (5 lb)

Wash the blackcurrants. Wash and stone the cherries, removing the stalks.

Put the blackcurrants into a preserving pan with the water. Simmer very gently for 20–30 minutes. Strain through a jelly bag for 2–3 hours.

Put the cherries into the pan and cover with the blackcurrant juice. Simmer for 10 minutes.

Add the sugar and stir over a moderate heat until dissolved. Bring to the boil and boil rapidly for about 10 minutes, stirring occasionally, or until setting point is reached.

Pot the jam in warm, clean jars and cover. Seal immediately.

Fresh Peach Jam

This jam is as lovely as it sounds – delicate, with the soft texture of peach flesh and slightly sharp with the lemon juice. You could also infuse a rose geranium leaf in it during the cooking to give a special fragrance. Try sandwiching a sponge cake with this jam – served with whipped cream, it makes a perfect dessert.

900 g (2 lb) ripe peaches
150 ml (¼ pint) water
90 ml (6 tbsp) lemon juice
1.4 kg (3 lb) sugar
225 ml (8 fl oz) pectin

MAKES 2.3 kg (5 lb)

Skin, stone and slice the peaches. Put into a preserving pan with the water and lemon juice. Simmer gently for 10–15 minutes until tender.

Add the sugar and stir over a moderate heat until dissolved. Bring to the boil and boil rapidly for 10 minutes, stirring occasionally.

Remove from the heat, stir in the pectin and then bring back to a steady boil for a further 5 minutes.

Allow to cool for a few minutes. Pot the jam in warm, clean jars and cover. Seal immediately.

Hedgerow Jam

Berrying and nutting in the late days of summer, as warm days give way to autumnal mists, have provided me with many contented moments. This jam, which is a rich combination of wild fruits and nuts, all harvested for free along a country walk, makes a delightful addition to the larder shelf.

450 g (1 lb) elderberries
450 g (1 lb) crabapples
450 g (1 lb) blackberries
450 g (1 lb) wild plums
  (bullaces or damsons)
225 g (8 oz) shelled
  hazelnuts

100 g (4 oz) shelled
  walnuts
1.7 litres (3 pints) water
2.3 kg (5 lb) sugar

MAKES 3.6 kg (8 lb)

Strip the elderberries off their stalks and rinse. Wash, core and chop the crabapples. Hull and rinse the blackberries. Wash, stone and chop the wild plums. Coarsely chop the nuts.

Put the fruit into a preserving pan with the water. Simmer for 15 minutes.

Add the sugar and stir over a moderate heat until dissolved. Bring to the boil and boil rapidly. After 5 minutes, add the nuts and continue boiling for about 10 minutes, stirring occasionally, or until setting point is reached.

Skim the jam if necessary, pot in warm, clean jars and cover. Seal while still hot.

Jam of Green Figs

Fresh figs always strike me as being the most luscious of fruits – warm with sunshine, dripping with juice and soft in texture. Their delicate and quite distinctive taste makes a marvellous, thick jam, as good on breads and scones as in desserts and tarts.

700 g (1½ lb) ripe green figs	rind and juice of 2 lemons
900 g (2 lb) rhubarb	
1.4 kg (3 lb) sugar	MAKES 2.7 kg (6 lb)

Wipe the figs and remove the stems, then roughly chop. Rinse and cut the rhubarb into 2.5 cm (1 inch) lengths.

Put the figs and rhubarb in a double boiler and cover with the sugar. Put on the lid and cook over boiling water for about 30–40 minutes until the sugar has dissolved in the juices and the fruit is quite soft.

Transfer the mixture to a preserving pan with the lemon rind and juice, stirring well. Bring to the boil and boil rapidly for about 10 minutes, stirring occasionally, or until setting point is reached.

Pot the jam in warm, clean jars and cover. Seal immediately.

Cherry and Apricot Jam

If you can lay your hands on a little gadget that stones cherries and other small fruits, it will take much of the drudgery out of making this jam and will encourage you to take full advantage of the cherry crop while it is in full season. I love apricots in jam, and this delightful combination of fruit is superlative.

450 g (1 lb) cherries	1.4 kg (3 lb) sugar
900 g (2 lb) apricots	juice of 2 lemons
150 ml (¼ pint) water	
	MAKES 2.3 kg (5 lb)

Wash and stone the cherries, removing the stalks. Wash, stone and slice the apricots.

Put the cherries and apricots into a preserving pan with the water and simmer for about 10–12 minutes until the fruit is tender.

Add the sugar and lemon juice and stir over a gentle heat until the sugar has dissolved. Bring to the boil and boil rapidly for about 10 minutes, stirring occasionally, or until setting point is reached.

Pot the jam in warm, clean jars and cover. Seal immediately.

DRIED APRICOT AND ALMOND JAM (page 20)

Dried Apricot and Almond Jam

A great favourite with family and friends alike, this is a jam of great sophistication and yet so simple to make. The flavour of the almonds comes through in a subtle yet amazing way and, of course, their crunch is in delectable contrast to the soft, sweet apricots. It also has a translucent quality which makes it even more appetising.

700 g (1½ lb) dried apricot halves	juice of 2 lemons
2.3 litres (4 pints) water	900 g (2 lb) sugar
75 g (3 oz) almonds	MAKES 2.3 kg (5 lb)

Rinse the apricots and soak overnight in the water. Drain the apricots, reserving the soaking water, and roughly chop. Roughly chop the almonds.

Grease a preserving pan with buttered paper, then add the apricots, soaking water and lemon juice. Simmer for 20 minutes, stirring frequently.

Add the sugar and stir over a medium heat until dissolved. Stir in the almonds, bring to the boil and boil rapidly for about 10 minutes, stirring occasionally, or until setting point is reached.

Pot the jam in warm, clean jars and cover. Seal immediately.

Pear and Ginger Jam

This is a jam of finesse, unbeatable on slices of freshly baked bread. The touch of hot spiciness in the ginger is in perfect balance with the delicacy of the pears, and makes a truly elegant and original jam. It has a thin, runny texture which is a part of its charm.

900 g (2 lb) pears	25 g (1 oz) fresh root ginger
100 g (4 oz) preserved stem ginger	juice of 2 lemons
900 g (2 lb) sugar	
300 ml (½ pint) water	MAKES 900 g (2 lb)

Peel, core and dice the pears. Cut the stem ginger into small chunks.

Put all the ingredients into a preserving pan and stir over a gentle heat until the sugar has dissolved. Bring to the boil and boil rapidly for about 10 minutes, stirring occasionally, or until setting point is reached.

Remove the piece of root ginger, lift out the fruit with a slotted spoon and place in warm, clean jars. Rapidly boil the syrup to reduce for a few minutes, then pour over the fruit to cover. Leave to cool. Cover and seal when cold.

Carrot and Almond Jam

Most people are astonished at the idea of carrots in jam, but it was a common practice in the 19th century. Mrs Beeton used to make it as an imitation apricot jam. Its sweetness and bright colouring make a perfect jam, and the taste and texture of almonds give this recipe extra flavour and crunch. The jam will not keep without the addition of the brandy – which has the pleasing side-effect of lifting it into the realms of the extra-special.

900 g (2 lb) carrots	grated rind of 2 lemons
100 g (4 oz) whole almonds	juice of 4 lemons
1.4 kg (3 lb) sugar	60 ml (4 tbsp) brandy

MAKES 2.3 kg (5 lb)

Wash and scrape the carrots. Put them through the coarse blades of a mincer or food processor. Chop the almonds.

Put the carrots into a saucepan of boiling water and cook for 15–20 minutes.

Drain and blend to a purée with a little of the cooking water.

Put the carrot purée into a preserving pan with the sugar, lemon rind and juice, stirring until the sugar has dissolved. Simmer gently for 5 minutes until the mixture begins to thicken. Stir in the almonds and brandy.

Pot the jam in warm, clean jars and cover. Seal immediately.

Scented Lychee Jam

Exotic tropical fruits are so easily available nowadays that it is rather fun to make preserves with them for a change. Lychees have a beautiful texture and colour, and their delicacy of taste is highlighted here by the flavour of rose geranium leaves and a few almonds.

700 g (1½ lb) fresh lychees	75 ml (2½ fl oz) water
3 rose geranium leaves	50 g (2 oz) slivered almonds
450 g (1 lb) sugar	
juice of 1 lemon	MAKES 900 g (2 lb)

Shell and stone the lychees. Tie the rose geranium leaves in a muslin bag.

Put all the ingredients into a preserving pan. Stir over a moderate heat until the sugar has dissolved. Bring to the boil and boil rapidly for about 10 minutes to a thick syrup, stirring frequently. Continue boiling for about 10 minutes, stirring occasionally, or until setting point is reached.

Pot the jam in warm, clean jars and cover. Seal.

Raisin, Date and Banana Jam

This is a tour de force, a really gastronomic assembling of ingredients which combine to make a fantastic jam. It is wonderful with breakfast toast, lovely in almond pastry slices and delicious spread on pancakes. A must for the store cupboard.

225 g (8 oz) dried apricots	450 g (1 lb) bananas, weight when peeled
450 g (1 lb) raisins	1.8 kg (4 lb) sugar
450 g (1 lb) dates	
	MAKES 2.3 kg (5 lb)

Rinse the apricots. Cover the raisins and apricots with water and soak overnight. Stone and chop the dates. Slice the bananas.

Put all the fruit into a preserving pan, with the soaking water. Simmer for 15 minutes.

Add the sugar and stir over a moderate heat until dissolved. Bring to the boil and boil rapidly for about 10 minutes, stirring occasionally, or until setting point is reached.

Pot the jam in warm, clean jars and cover. Seal.

MELON AND PINEAPPLE JAM (page 24)

Melon and Pineapple Jam

Two tropical fruits, with the addition of lemon juice to provide extra flavour, make this translucent and succulent jam. Pale golden and gleaming, it is a beautiful sight amongst a range of preserves in the pantry. I use this jam a great deal in desserts of all kinds.

900 g (2 lb) honeydew melon, weight after preparation	juice of 3 lemons
	1.4 kg (3 lb) sugar
700 g (1½ lb) fresh pineapple	MAKES 2.3 kg (5 lb)

Cut the melon in half, scoop out the seeds and cut the flesh into small cubes, weighing out 900 g (2 lb). Remove the skin from the pineapple and cut out the central core, then cut the flesh into small chunks.

Put the melon and pineapple into a preserving pan with the lemon juice. Simmer gently for 10–15 minutes until tender.

Add the sugar and stir over a moderate heat until dissolved. Bring to the boil and boil rapidly for about 10 minutes, stirring occasionally, or until setting point is reached.

Pot the jam in warm, clean jars and cover. Seal while still hot.

Apricot, Walnut and Pineapple Jam

I love nuts in jam. It is not just their contrasting texture, but also the fact that the cooking at high temperature brings out the finest in their taste. Pineapple makes a marvellous jam – silky and transparent and, in combination with apricots, makes a jam to remember.

450 g (1 lb) ripe apricots	100 g (4 oz) walnut pieces
450 g (1 lb) sugar	
225 g (8 oz) can pineapple chunks, in fruit juice	MAKES 1–1.4 kg (2–3 lb)

Rinse, stone and halve the apricots. Place in a bowl and cover them with the sugar. Leave to stand for 2 hours.

Meanwhile, crack the stones and remove the kernels. Drain the pineapple chunks and reserve the juice. Chop the walnuts.

Put the apricots, sugar and pineapple juice into a preserving pan and gradually bring to the boil, stirring constantly and skimming as necessary.

Add the pineapple chunks, kernels and walnuts. Simmer very gently for about 10 minutes, stirring occasionally, or until setting point is reached.

Pot the jam in warm, clean jars and cover. Seal while hot.

Banana and Dried Fig Jam

I was fascinated to try this unusual mixture of fresh and dried fruit. My experiment was richly rewarded by an exotic, thickly textured jam which turned out to be utterly scrumptious – quite irresistible on the tea-table, and now a regular feature in my store cupboard.

4 lemons	150 ml (¼ pint) water
1.6 kg (3½ lb) bananas	1.4 kg (3 lb) sugar
225 g (8 oz) dried figs	
	MAKES 2.3 kg (5 lb)

Peel the rind and pith from the lemons. Remove the pips and put the pips and pith in a muslin bag. Peel and slice the bananas into 5 mm (¼ inch) slices. Chop the figs.

Put the banana slices into a bowl with the water and the juice of two of the lemons. Add the bag of pips and the figs. Cover with the sugar and leave to stand for 24 hours.

Transfer the banana mixture to a preserving pan and heat gently until the sugar has dissolved. Bring to the boil and boil rapidly for about 10 minutes, stirring occasionally, or until setting point is reached. Remove the muslin bag.

Pot the jam in warm, clean jars and cover. Seal immediately.

Marrow, Pineapple and Ginger Jam

This golden jam, which gleams as the light shines through it, has been a family favourite for years. It is wonderfully, even unashamedly, sweet, yet the ginger counteracts this with its characteristic bite. This jam is a marvellous filling for cakes and crêpes as well as being the devil's own temptation on fresh bread.

2.7 kg (6 lb) marrow, weight when prepared	225 g (8 oz) stem ginger
	2.7 kg (6 lb) sugar
450 g (1 lb) pineapple, weight when prepared	
	MAKES 4.5 kg (10 lb)

Skin, deseed and cut the marrow into small cubes. Cut the skin off the pineapple, remove the central core and cut the flesh into little chunks. Slice the ginger.

Mix the marrow and pineapple together and make alternating layers of fruit and sugar in a preserving pan. Leave overnight to extract the juice.

Bring to the boil and boil rapidly for 15–20 minutes to reduce the liquid. Add the ginger and boil rapidly for about 10 minutes, stirring occasionally, or until setting point is reached.

Pot the jam in warm, clean jars and cover. Seal.

Rosy Tomato Jam

The unusual combination of tomatoes and lemons makes a jam with a quite distinctive character – although it's not really a jam at all, more like a relish. I like to use it in toasted cheese sandwiches – it transforms them!

5 lemons, washed	knob of butter
150 ml (¼ pint) water	
1 kg (2 lb) red tomatoes	MAKES 1.5 kg (3 lb)
1 kg (2 lb) sugar	

Cut the lemons in half and squeeze the juice, reserving the pips. Remove the remaining flesh from the lemon halves and reserve. Cut the excess pith away from the lemon rind and cut the rind into thin strips. Place in a saucepan, add the water and simmer, covered, for 20 minutes.

Skin and quarter the tomatoes then remove the cores and seeds and tie in a piece of muslin with the lemon pips and flesh. Measure the lemon juice, make it up to 1.8 litres (3 pints) with water and pour into a preserving pan. Coarsely chop the tomato flesh and add to the pan with the softened lemon shreds, liquid and muslin bag. Simmer gently for about 40 minutes until tender. Remove the muslin bag and squeeze it well, allowing the juice to run back into the pan. Remove the pan from the heat, add the sugar, stirring until dissolved then add a knob of butter and boil rapidly for 20 minutes or until setting point is reached. Take the pan off the heat and remove any scum with a slotted spoon. Pot the jam in warm, clean jars and cover. Seal immediately.

Blueberry Jam

The prettiness of this jam is immensely appealing – the berries just manage to hold their shape and not become too pulpy, and the jam is scrumptious with freshly baked bread at tea time. So when the blueberry is available, make the most of it and enjoy this jam!

1.25 kg (2½ lb) blueberries	knob of butter
150 ml (¼ pint) water	225 ml (8 fl oz) pectin
45 ml (3 tbsp) lemon juice	MAKES ABOUT 2.75 kg (5½ lb)
1.5 kg (3 lb) sugar	

Wash the blueberries then put them into a preserving pan with the water and lemon juice. Simmer gently for 10–15 minutes until the fruit is soft and just beginning to pulp. Remove the pan from the heat, add the sugar, stir until dissolved, then add a knob of butter. Bring to the boil and boil rapidly for 3 minutes. Remove the pan from the heat, add the pectin, return to the heat and boil for a further minute. Allow to cool slightly before potting the jam in warm, clean jars. Cover and seal while still hot.

Jellies

I ALWAYS think that making jellies is simpler than any other preserve-making, so long as you have a jelly bag and a thermometer! You don't have to skin or core or top and tail the fruits, and the basic rules about the ratio of juice to sugar remain constant, so after a while you can do it almost automatically. Jellies look so beautiful in the jars, too, translucent and shining, all with delicate colours whether pale or dark. Jellies can be used to go with both savoury and sweet recipes, and are perennially useful and popular with young and old alike. And you can make a jelly from almost anything – from tomatoes to rose-hips, green peppers to blackberries, and all are delicious.

➤ SPECIAL EQUIPMENT ➤

In addition to the basic equipment needed for jam-making, (see page 10), you will need a jelly bag or a linen cloth for straining the juice from the cooked fruit. Cleanliness is paramount at this stage: always scald the cloth or the jelly bag in boiling water before use, then wring it dry. The traditional way to suspend a cloth or jelly bag is to use an upturned kitchen chair. To do this, tie the four corners of the linen cloth very securely (because of the weight of the fruit and water) to the four legs. Place a bowl underneath and allow the juice to drip through, undisturbed, for 12 hours. With a jelly bag, tie the suspending tapes to the bar of the chair. Do not be tempted to squeeze the bag in order to extract the maximum juice – this will turn the jelly cloudy.

➤ BASIC METHOD ➤

Make sure that the fruit you are using is clean, and not over-ripe. Remove any stalks but it is not necessary to top and tail berries such as gooseberries and currants. Pick the fruit over and discard any mouldy or over-ripe ones. It is best to pick the fruit on a dry day, because fruit sodden with rain will attract mildew. Rinse the fruit to remove any dirt or grit; the fruit is then ready to cook as instructed in the recipe.

The juice is then strained through the scalded jelly bag or linen cloth (see left), and measured. The general rule for jellies is to add 450 g (1 lb) sugar to every 600 ml (1 pint) juice. This gives a jelly which will both set and keep, although this ratio varies slightly in recipes for different fruits. Stir over a medium heat until dissolved then bring to the boil and boil fast to setting point. This will take about 10 minutes, longer if the fruit has a high water content. As a guide, about 4.5 kg (10 lb) jelly will result from every 2.7 kg (6 lb) sugar used.

Skim the jelly with a metal spoon and remove the last traces of scum with a piece of absorbent kitchen paper. A thick, fairly sticky juice is sure to contain plenty of pectin, but the testing for set is the same as that for jam (see page 12). Pour immediately into warm, clean jars, before it has a chance to set in the pan. Cover at once with waxed discs, waxed side down, and then with a cellophane disc (this you can do when it is either hot or cold). Be careful not to tilt the jars until the jelly has set. Store in a cool, dry, dark place.

Suitable Fruits for Jelly-Making

Windfall apples, barberries, blackberries – both red and ripe, blackcurrants, cherries, gooseberries, raspberries, strawberries, crabapples, damsons or wild plums, elderberries, haws, japonica, loganberries, medlars, mulberries, plums, pears, quinces, red and white currants, rowan, sloes, rose-hips, oranges.

Flavourings for Jellies

Aromatic leaves and petals give a delicate and unusual flavour to jellies – for example a scented geranium leaf gives apple jelly a beautiful taste and aroma. You can use peach leaves for their almondy flavour, lemon verbena for its lemony perfume, red scented rose petals, mint leaves, angelica leaves or stem – all add their distinctive and characteristic flavours to make a jelly with a difference. As a general rule, use one highly scented leaf or a small handful of petals to each 600 ml (1 pint) juice – in both cases tied in a muslin bag and suspended from the pan handle while the jelly is boiling to setting point.

Making Jelly in a Pressure Cooker

To save time, you can cook the fruit for making jellies in a pressure cooker, as indeed you can with jams. First wash the fruit, then put it into the cooker, making sure that it does not fill up to more than halfway. As a general rule, pressure cook berries at 4.5 kg (10 lb) for 5 minutes. Fruits such as medlars and rose hips will need 30 minutes, whereas apples will take only 8 minutes. Follow your cooker's instructions.

Mash the fruit, then strain through a jelly bag in the normal way. Continue the cooking process as for the preserving pan technique on page 12.

Serving Ideas

Jellies make a tasty accompaniment to roast meats both hot and cold, and certain ones are delicious with cheeses. A ploughman's lunch is enhanced by a selection of sweet and sharp jellies, and they go beautifully with cream cheese, too. Fold a scented jelly into yogurt to flavour it.

Quantities

Exact quantities of jelly vary with the water content of the fruit and the length of time needed to cook them. As a general rule, 4.5 kg (10 lb) jelly is made from each 2.7 kg (6 lb) sugar used.

Blackcurrant Jelly

The strong, rich taste of blackcurrants makes, to my mind, the king of jellies. A beautiful dark red, almost black, in colour, it is so versatile too – you can use blackcurrant jelly in puddings and pies, as a spread, or with cold meals. An essential standby for a well stocked larder.

1.8 kg (4 lb) ripe blackcurrants	600 ml (1 pint) water sugar

Wash and strip the blackcurrants off their stalks but do not top and tail them.

Put the blackcurrants into a preserving pan with the water. Cover and simmer for 30 minutes, crushing the fruit from time to time with the back of a wooden spoon. Allow to cool a little in the pan, then strain through a jelly bag overnight.

Measure the juice into the cleaned preserving pan. To every 600 ml (1 pint) juice, add 450 g (1 lb) sugar. Stir over a gentle heat until the sugar has dissolved. Bring to the boil and boil rapidly for about 10 minutes, stirring occasionally, or until setting point is reached, removing the scum as it forms on the surface.

Pour the jelly into warm, clean jars and cover. Seal immediately.

Apricot Muscatel Jelly

The unusual idea of including muscatel raisins in jelly-making works very well. They add their distinctive taste to that of the apricots, making a jelly that is as delicious in savoury as in sweet dishes.

450 g (1 lb) dried apricots	150 ml (¼ pint) muscat d'Alsace
100 g (4 oz) muscatel raisins	sugar
1.7 litres (3 pints) water	175 ml (6 fl oz) pectin
juice of 2 lemons	

Rinse the apricots and raisins. Cover them with the water and leave to soak for 48 hours.

Put the apricots and raisins into a preserving pan with the soaking water and lemon juice. Simmer for about 25 minutes until the fruit is very soft. Strain through a jelly bag overnight.

Add the wine to the juice and measure into the cleaned preserving pan. To every 600 ml (1 pint) juice, add 450 g (1 lb) sugar. Stir over a gentle heat until the sugar has dissolved. Bring to the boil and boil rapidly for 10 minutes. Add the pectin and stir in thoroughly.

Skim if necessary, pour the jelly into warm, clean jars and cover. Seal immediately.

Cranberry Wine Jelly

This is a bright red jelly in the classical style, beautifully sharp and an excellent foil for rich meats such as lamb or game birds.

900 g (2 lb) cranberries	sugar
300 ml (½ pint) water	300 ml (½ pint) claret

Wash the cranberries. Put into a preserving pan with the water. Cover and simmer gently for about 25 minutes, until tender. Strain through a jelly bag overnight.

Measure the juice into the cleaned preserving pan. To every 600 ml (1 pint) juice, add 350 g (12 oz) sugar. Stir over a gentle heat until the sugar has dissolved. Add the wine. Bring to the boil and boil rapidly for about 10 minutes, stirring occasionally, or until setting point is reached.

Skim, pour the jelly into warm, clean jars and cover. Seal immediately.

Grape Burgundy Jelly

The delicate flavour of grapes makes a lovely jelly, and the touch of red wine gives this luxury recipe a certain quality, as well as a beautiful magenta colour. It is delicious on fresh bread or toast, and is also an interesting accompaniment to hot roast meats.

700 g (1½ lb) ripe black grapes	150 ml (¼ pint) Burgundy red wine
300 ml (½ pint) water	225 ml (8 fl oz) pectin
sugar	
30 ml (2 tbsp) lemon juice	MAKES 1.4 kg (3 lb)

Wash, deseed and crush the grapes, about 225 g (8 oz) at a time, in a food processor for a few seconds.

Put the grapes into a preserving pan with the water. Cover and simmer for 20 minutes. Strain through a jelly bag overnight.

Measure the juice into the cleaned preserving pan. To every 600 ml (1 pint) juice, add 350 g (12 oz) sugar. Stir in the lemon juice and wine. Stir over a gentle heat until the sugar has dissolved. Bring to the boil and simmer for 15 minutes. Remove from the heat and stir in the pectin. Skim if necessary, pour the jelly into warm, clean jars and cover. Seal.

MANY BERRY JELLY (page 36)

Blackberry and Gooseberry Jelly

This unusual mixture of late summer fruits makes a really wonderful dark red jelly. Delicious at breakfast time, it gets the day off to a flying start!

900 g (2 lb) blackberries	**450 ml (¾ pint) water**
450 g (1 lb) gooseberries	**sugar**

Rinse the blackberries and gooseberries. Put the fruit into a preserving pan with the water. Cover and simmer for 30–40 minutes until completely soft. Strain through a jelly bag overnight.

Measure the juice into the cleaned preserving pan. To every 600 ml (1 pint) juice, add 450 g (1 lb) sugar. Stir over a gentle heat until the sugar has dissolved. Bring to the boil and boil rapidly for about 10 minutes, stirring occasionally, or until setting point is reached.

Skim, pour the jelly into warm, clean jars and cover. Seal immediately.

Mulberry Jelly

The mulberry is an exquisite fruit, dripping with deep red juice which stains the fingers like ink. It is, however, full of pips so making a jelly is the obvious and best way to make the most of its unique flavour.

450 g (1 lb) mulberries	**150 ml (¼ pint) water**
1 large cooking apple	**sugar**

Rinse the mulberries. Wash and chop the apple. Put the fruit into a preserving pan with the water. Cover and simmer gently for 30 minutes until the fruit is very soft. Strain the fruit mixture through a jelly bag overnight.

Measure the juice into the cleaned preserving pan. To every 600 ml (1 pint) juice, add 450 g (1 lb) sugar. Stir over a gentle heat until the sugar has dissolved. Bring to the boil and boil rapidly for about 10 minutes, stirring occasionally, or until setting point is reached.

Skim, pour the jelly into warm, clean jars and cover. Seal immediately.

Raspberry Jelly

Nothing can beat home-made raspberry jelly on a tea-table piled high with fresh scones and newly baked bread. So when raspberries reach their peak in the summer, this is one of the nicest ways to preserve them.

1.8 kg (4 lb) raspberries
600 ml (1 pint) water
sugar

Hull and rinse the raspberries. Put into a preserving pan with the water. Cover and simmer gently for 25 minutes. Allow to cool a little in the pan, then strain through a jelly bag overnight.

Measure the juice into the cleaned preserving pan. To every 600 ml (1 pint) juice, add 350 g (12 oz) sugar. Stir over a moderate heat until the sugar has dissolved. Bring to the boil and boil rapidly for about 10 minutes, stirring occasionally, or until setting point is reached.

Skim, pour the jelly into warm, clean jars and cover. Seal while still hot.

Satsuma and Grapefruit Jelly

This wonderful citrus jelly is a clear, pale gold in colour and has a sharp, clean taste which personally I love. For those who enjoy slightly bitter flavours, this is gorgeous on toast, and superlative with hot roast chicken or other poultry.

2 grapefruit   1 lemon
2 satsumas   sugar

Wash and coarsely chop the fruit. Put into a preserving pan with water to cover. Cover and simmer for 2 hours. Strain through a jelly bag overnight.

Measure the juice into the cleaned preserving pan. To every 600 ml (1 pint) juice, add 450 g (1 lb) sugar. Stir over a gentle heat until the sugar has dissolved. Bring to the boil and boil rapidly for about 10 minutes, stirring occasionally, or until setting point is reached.

Pour the jelly into warm, clean jars and cover. Seal immediately.

Exotic Fruit Jelly

Now that the shops are full of tropical fruits, it is fun to ring the changes and branch out from traditional jelly-making. Selections from any of these exotic fruits will make a range of fragrant and interesting jellies. Use a selection of some of the following:

nectarines, mangoes, guavas, papayas, lychees, kiwifruit, persimmons, ogen melons, pineapple	sugar lemon juice

Rinse and prepare all the fruit. For example, quarter the nectarines, mangoes, guavas and papayas (you can leave the stones and pips in); peel the lychees and kiwifruit; chop the persimmons; scoop out the flesh from the melons and pineapple, then roughly chop.

Put the fruit into a preserving pan with water to cover. Cover and simmer for 30 minutes. Strain through a jelly bag overnight.

Measure the juice into the cleaned preserving pan. To every 600 ml (1 pint) juice, add 450 g (1 lb) sugar and 15 ml (1 tbsp) lemon juice. Stir over a gentle heat until the sugar has dissolved. Bring to the boil and boil rapidly for about 10 minutes, stirring occasionally, or until setting point is reached.

Pour the jelly into warm, clean jars and cover. Seal while still hot.

Rose Petal Jelly

Scented rose petals give a fantastic flavour to a fruit jelly – it is a pity that we do not use them more than we do in cooking. They did in the old days and for good reason: they make something very special out of something very simple.

900 g (2 lb) cooking apples	50 g (2 oz) dark red scented rose petals
750 ml (1¼ pints) water	sugar
juice of 1 lemon	

Wash and roughly chop the apples. Put into a preserving pan with 600 ml (1 pint) of the water and the lemon juice. Cover and simmer gently for about 30 minutes until pulpy. Strain through a jelly bag overnight.

Meanwhile, cut the triangular white base from the rose petals and discard. Put the petals into the pan with the remaining water. Cover and simmer for 15 minutes. Strain through a jelly bag separately, or use a clean linen or muslin cloth.

Mix the two juices together and measure them into the cleaned preserving pan. To every 600 ml (1 pint) juice, add 350 g (12 oz) sugar. Stir over a gentle heat until the sugar has dissolved. Bring to the boil and boil rapidly for about 10 minutes, stirring occasionally, or until setting point is reached.

Skim, pour the jelly into warm, clean jars and cover. Seal immediately.

ROSE PETAL JELLY (above)

Many Berry Jelly

When the soft fruit harvest is at its peak, this is a gorgeous way of combining them – their tastes mingle and yet are not lost. This is a jelly to remind you of long summer days later on in the year when these fruits are no longer around.

Equal quantities of
cherries
raspberries
strawberries
gooseberries
sugar

Wash and stone the cherries, removing the stalks. Hull and rinse the raspberries and strawberries. Wash the gooseberries. Put the fruit into a large strong bowl. Cover with a plate and weigh it down with a heavy bowl or something similar to crush the fruit. Leave overnight.

Put the fruit into a preserving pan with all the extracted juice and water to cover. Simmer for 10 minutes. Strain through a jelly bag overnight.

Measure the juice into the cleaned preserving pan. To every 600 ml (1 pint) juice, add 350 g (12 oz) sugar. Stir over a gentle heat until the sugar has dissolved. Bring to the boil and boil rapidly for about 10 minutes, stirring occasionally, or until setting point is reached.

Skim, pour the jelly into warm, clean jars and cover. Seal immediately.

Guava Jelly

Tropical guavas make a beautiful soft pink jelly, which looks lovely amongst a range of multicoloured jams and jellies on the larder shelf.

guavas
sugar
lime juice

Wash and cut the guavas into quarters. Put into a preserving pan with enough water just to cover. Cover and simmer for 30 minutes. Strain through a jelly bag overnight.

Measure the juice back into the cleaned preserving pan. To every 600 ml (1 pint) juice, add 350 g (12 oz) sugar and 15 ml (1 tbsp) lime juice. Stir over a medium heat until the sugar has dissolved. Bring to the boil and boil rapidly for about 10 minutes, stirring occasionally, or until setting point is reached.

Skim, pour the jelly into warm, clean jars and cover. Seal immediately.

Red and White Currant Jelly

This fine jelly has a delicate flavour and lovely deep pink colour. It goes particularly well with game birds, its strength and sharpness providing the perfect balance to their richness.

1.4 kg (3 lb) white currants	900 ml (1½ pints) water
1.4 kg (3 lb) redcurrants	sugar

Strip the currants from the stalks and place in a colander. Gently rinse under cold running water and shake thoroughly to drain.

Put the fruit into a preserving pan with the water. Bring slowly to the boil, mashing the fruit occasionally with the back of a wooden spoon to break it up. Cover and simmer gently for 30 minutes. Strain through a jelly bag overnight.

Measure the juice into the cleaned preserving pan. To every 600 ml (1 pint) juice, add 450 g (1 lb) sugar. Stir over a gentle heat until the sugar has dissolved. Bring to the boil and boil rapidly for about 10 minutes, stirring occasionally, or until setting point is reached.

Skim, pour the jelly into warm, clean jars and cover. Seal immediately.

Medlar Jelly

The medlar is a curious fruit, unpromising to look at – rather like a large, russet-coloured rose-hip with rough, leathery skin – but much used in the past by the country housewife as part of her wild harvest. Making jelly with these quince-like fruits is the best way of using them.

1.8 kg (4 lb) medlars	900 ml (1½ pints) water
4 lemons	sugar

Wash and roughly chop the medlars. Peel the lemons and squeeze the juice. Put the lemon rinds into a preserving pan with the medlars and water. Cover and simmer for 1 hour until the fruit is thoroughly softened. Strain through a jelly bag overnight.

Measure the juice into the cleaned preserving pan. To every 600 ml (1 pint) juice, add 450 g (1 lb) sugar. Add the lemon juice. Stir over a gentle heat until the sugar has dissolved. Bring to the boil and boil rapidly for about 10 minutes, stirring occasionally, or until setting point is reached.

Skim, pour the jelly into warm, clean jars and cover. Seal while still hot.

Crab Apple and Thyme Jelly

A sharp, aromatic jelly in which the thyme gives its pungent flavour and aroma to a sharp, clear red jelly. It is delicious with the Christmas turkey as a change from the traditional cranberry jelly.

1.4 kg (3 lb) crab apples
large bunch of thyme
sugar

Wash the crab apples. Put in a preserving pan with water to cover and the thyme. Cover and simmer for 40 minutes. Strain through a jelly bag overnight.

Measure the juice into the cleaned preserving pan. To every 600 ml (1 pint) juice, add 450 g (1 lb) sugar. Stir over a gentle heat until the sugar has dissolved. Bring to the boil and boil rapidly for about 10 minutes, stirring occasionally, or until setting point is reached.

Skim, pour the jelly into warm, clean jars and cover. Seal immediately.

Rose Geranium and Orange Jelly

The simple device of adding a scented leaf to fruit while it is cooking gives an utterly distinctive flavour and aroma to jelly. Rose geranium with orange is one of the most exquisite of combinations.

900 g (2 lb) oranges
900 ml (1½ pints) water
4–5 rose geranium leaves

sugar
225 ml (8 fl oz) pectin

Wash and halve the oranges. Squeeze the juice, then roughly chop the fruit. Put into a preserving pan with the water. Cover and simmer for 1½–2 hours until the rind is soft, adding the rose geranium leaves for the last 10 minutes of the cooking. Strain through the jelly bag overnight, leaving the leaves in the pulp.

Measure the juice into the cleaned preserving pan. To every 600 ml (1 pint) juice, add 450 g (1 lb) sugar. Stir over a gentle heat until the sugar has dissolved. Bring to the boil and boil rapidly for 15 minutes. Remove from the heat, add the pectin and stir well.

Skim if necessary, pour the jelly into warm, clean jars and cover. Seal immediately.

CRAB APPLE AND THYME JELLY (above)

Sage and Apple Jelly

Herb jellies make marvellous companions to meat dishes, both hot and cold. This combination of sage and apple goes particularly well with pork.

900 g (2 lb) cooking apples	pared rind and juice of 1 lemon
large bunch of fresh sage	sugar

Wash and roughly chop the apples. Put into a preserving pan with water to cover, the bunch of sage, lemon rind and juice. Cover and simmer for about 30 minutes until the fruit is very soft. Strain the fruit mixture through a jelly bag overnight.

Measure the juice into the cleaned preserving pan. To every 600 ml (1 pint) juice, add 450 g (1 lb) sugar. Stir over a gentle heat until the sugar has dissolved. Bring to the boil and boil rapidly for about 10 minutes, stirring occasionally, or until setting point is reached.

Skim, pour the jelly into warm, clean jars and cover. Seal while still hot.

Pear and Rosemary Jelly

This is a delicate and beautifully balanced jelly. They say that rosemary is for remembrance and this is definitely a taste to remember!

900 g (2 lb) pears	sugar
pared rind and juice of 2 lemons	225 ml (8 fl oz) pectin
medium bunch of rosemary	

Wash and remove the stalks from the pears and chop the fruit roughly. Put into a preserving pan with the lemon rind and juice and bunch of rosemary. Add enough water to just cover the fruit. Cover and simmer for 25–30 minutes until the pears are very soft. Strain through a jelly bag overnight.

Measure the juice into the cleaned preserving pan. To every 600 ml (1 pint) juice, add 450 g (1 lb) sugar. Stir over a gentle heat until the sugar has dissolved. Bring to the boil and boil rapidly for 10 minutes. Remove from the heat and stir in the pectin.

Skim if necessary, pour the jelly into warm, clean jars and cover. Seal immediately.

Mint Jelly

This famous sauce was, so some say, invented by the Romans to go with roast lamb – both to counteract its richness and to complement its taste. Whoever's idea it was, it has lasted and become a classic of English cookery.

2.5 kg (5 lb) cooking apples	sugar
1.2 litres (2 pints) water	90–120 ml (6–8 tbsp) chopped fresh mint
few sprigs of fresh mint	few drops of green food colouring (optional)
1.2 litres (2 pints) white vinegar	

Wash the apples and remove any bruised or damaged portions. Roughly chop them into thick chunks without peeling or coring. Place them in a large saucepan with the water and mint sprigs. Bring to the boil, then simmer gently for about 45 minutes until soft and pulpy. Stir from time to time to prevent sticking. Add the vinegar and boil for a further 5 minutes.

Strain through a jelly bag overnight.

Measure the juice and put it in a preserving pan with 500 g (1 lb) sugar for each 600 ml (1 pint) juice. Stir over a gentle heat until the sugar has dissolved, then boil rapidly for about 10 minutes until setting point is reached. Take the pan off the heat and remove any scum with a slotted spoon. Stir in the chopped mint and add a few drops of green food colouring, if liked. Allow to cool slightly, then stir well to distribute the mint. Pour the jelly into warm, clean jars and cover. Seal immediately.

Bitter Lime Jelly with Pernod

This sophisticated and elegant jelly is a pièce de resistance and never fails to win admiring comments. Served with charcuterie as an hors d'oeuvre, it makes an original and mouthwatering start to a meal, and it is also excellent with roast game birds.

4 limes	sugar
3.6 litres (6 pints) water	15 ml (1 tbsp) Pernod

Wash the limes and roughly slice them. Put the limes in a preserving pan with the water and simmer gently for 1 hour until the fruit is soft. Strain through a jelly bag into a large bowl overnight.

Measure the extract and return it to the pan with 500 g (1 lb) sugar for each 600 ml (1 pint) extract. Stir over a gentle heat until the sugar has dissolved. Bring to the boil and boil rapidly for 10–15 minutes or until setting point is reached. Take the pan off the heat and stir in the Pernod. Remove any scum from the surface with a slotted spoon. Pour the jelly into warm, clean jars and cover. Seal immediately.

Marmalades

MARMALADE is one of the most British of conventions – although it gets its name from the Portuguese for a quince, 'marmelo', the fruit from which this conserve was originally made. Marmalade was made famous by the Keiller family in the 18th century and it was they who first had the idea of including strips of peel in the orange jam or jelly. In the 1870s a Mrs. Cooper, a grocer's wife from Oxford, started making marmalade on a commercial scale, a business which took her name and is now synonymous with the best of British breakfasts. However, there·are numerous delicious variations on the theme of orange marmalade to try out for yourself, as the following recipes demonstrate.

★ EXTRA EQUIPMENT ★

A food processor, with both coarse and fine cutters, is a great boon for making marmalade, although a mincer with a variety of blades does the job just as well, if not as quickly. A pressure cooker is also useful since citrus fruit skins need to be softened thoroughly and require 1½–2 hours open boiling: a pressure cooker can cut this time down to between 10–20 minutes. (A warning note: do not fill your pressure cooker more than half full with fruit.)

★ BASIC METHOD ★

Using the basic equipment for jam-making, follow the instructions in the individual recipes and, for best marmalade results, observe the following tips:

★ Do not boil the shredded rind or peel too rapidly, because this will harden and toughen them.

★ The process of boiling with sugar is crucial – underboiled marmalade is too thin and will not keep well whereas, if overboiled, it stiffens and thickens like toffee. So keep the boil continuous and steady for 10–15 minutes, then boil fast to setting point.

★ Most of the pectin, so necessary for a good set, is in the pith and pips of citrus fruits, rather than in the fruit pulp or juice, so these are important elements in the success of the marmalade-making process. They are usually tied up in a muslin bag and cooked with the fruit in order to extract the pectin and bring it into solution. It is a good idea to tie the bag to the pan handle so that you can remove it more easily before adding the sugar.

★ Citrus fruits for marmalade should be just ripe. When using oranges, try to obtain Sevilles when they are in season because they have an exceptional flavour.

★ If the recipe says to peel the fruit, soak it first for a couple of minutes in boiling water, and it will peel off more easily.

★ Use a very sharp knife for shredding if you are not using a mincer or food processor, and always cut smaller than you require in the end product since the rind swells slightly during cooking.

★ For a coarse-cut marmalade, you can boil the whole fruit for 2 hours first, and cut them in half and remove the pips. Cut up the fruit, retaining as much juice as possible, and return the pips to the water in which the fruit was first cooked. Boil for 5 minutes to extract the pectin, strain over the sliced fruit, add lemon juice and then continue the process of adding the sugar and cooking to setting point.

★ A jelly marmalade is made by boiling the shredded rind in a bag, keeping it separate from the main fruit mixture. This is then strained through a jelly bag and the liquid mixed with sugar and cooked to setting point with the addition of the shredded rind.

★ Always remove scum as soon as setting point is reached with a warm metal spoon. Leave the skimmed marmalade to cool until a thin skin begins to form on the surface, then stir gently to distribute the peel – if you do this, the peel will not rise to the top of the jar. If you are making jelly marmalades, however, leave them undisturbed.

★ Waxed discs should be placed on the top of the marmalade immediately, taking care to avoid any air bubbles forming underneath. Leave until cold, and then cover with the outer cellophane disc. This is to ensure that condensation does not occur underneath the disc, which would encourage the growth of moulds. Seal with a rubber band or plastic screw top. Wipe the jars clean with a damp cloth. Label attractively with the contents of the jar and the date. Store marmalade in a cool, dark, dry place.

PRESSURE COOKER METHOD

Put the cut or shredded rind or peel into the pressure cooker with the muslin bag of pips and pith. Add the water and cook at 4.5 kg (10 lb) pressure for 7–20 minutes (see table below). Open the cooker and remove the bag. Add the sugar and cook in the open cooker over a low heat until the sugar has dissolved. Bring to the boil and boil rapidly to setting point.

PRESSURE COOKER GUIDE

Cook at 4.5 kg (10 lb) pressure

GRAPEFRUIT	10 Minutes
LEMON	7
LIME	20
ORANGE JELLY MARMALADE	20
SEVILLE ORANGES	10
TANGERINES	12
ORANGES	7

Best Seville Marmalade

For all the hard work involved in making this marmalade, it is worth every minute – with its lovely deep brownish-orange colour, and a taste quite incomparable with any shop-bought variety. So put aside a couple of days in January, when Seville oranges are in season, and you will be rewarded at breakfast time for the rest of the year round!

2.3 kg (5 lb) Seville oranges
sugar

MAKES 4.5 kg (10 lb)

Wash and halve the oranges then squeeze the juice. Tie the pips in a muslin bag and soak them in 300 ml (½ pint) water for 30 minutes. Slice the orange skins very finely.

Put the pip bag in a preserving pan with the fruit. To every 450 g (1 lb) fruit, add 1.7 litres (3 pints) water. Add the juice and leave for 24 hours.

Simmer the fruit for about 2 hours until tender. Leave for a further 24 hours.

Weigh the fruit into the cleaned preserving pan. To every 450 g (1 lb) fruit, add 550 g (1¼ lb) sugar. Stir over a gentle heat to dissolve the sugar. Bring to the boil and boil rapidly for about 10 minutes, stirring occasionally, or until setting point is reached.

Pot in warm, clean jars. Cover and seal.

Thick Quince Marmalade

This is THE original marmalade, historically speaking, because the name 'marmalade' comes from the Portuguese 'marmelo', meaning a quince. A thick paste of quinces was a medieval delicacy, an early form of marmalade which was later modified by the addition of citrus fruits, then later still made without any quinces at all. But if you can get hold of quinces, this is well worth making. It is a deep orange-red in colour, thick in texture and quite individual in taste.

quinces
sugar

Wash, remove the stalks and slice the quinces. Put into a preserving pan and cover with water. Simmer gently for 40–50 minutes, stirring occasionally, until the fruit is very soft. Pass through a sieve to separate the pulp from the pips.

Weigh the pulp into the cleaned preserving pan. To every 450 g (1 lb) pulp, add 350 g (12 oz) sugar. Stir over a medium heat until the sugar has dissolved. Simmer gently for about 10 minutes or until setting point is reached, stirring to prevent the quinces burning.

Pot the marmalade in warm, clean jars. Cover and seal while still hot.

Fine-Cut Orange and Grapefruit Marmalade

The inclusion of grapefruit in marmalade is very refreshing – I love the fresh sharpness of this delicate marmalade. It is very simple and straightforward to make if you have a food processor to shred the rind. You can, of course, make this marmalade at any time of the year.

5 oranges	2.5 ml (½ tsp) bicarbonate
2 grapefruit	of soda
juice of 2 lemons	sugar
2.3 litres (4 pints) water	
	MAKES 2.7 kg (6 lb)

Wash the fruit and cut in half. Squeeze the juice, reserving the pips. Slice the rind very thinly. Alternatively shred the rind in a food processor. Tie the pips in a muslin bag.

Put the bag of pips in a small saucepan with the lemon juice. Just cover with water and bring to the boil. Strain into a preserving pan. Add the water, bicarbonate of soda and shredded rind. Simmer, partially covered, for 1½ hours until the fruit is soft.

Measure the fruit and juice, for every 600 ml (1 pint) add 450 g (1 lb) sugar. Stir over a medium heat until the sugar has dissolved. Bring to the boil and simmer for about 10 minutes, stirring occasionally, until setting point is reached.

Pot the marmalade in warm, clean jars. Cover and seal immediately.

Fine-Cut Green Tomato Marmalade

At the end of summer, when there are unripened tomatoes still on the vine with no hope of sun to turn them red, try making this delicate marmalade with its gingery flavour and exciting texture. Lovely on autumnal days, having tea in front of the first log fires of the colder weather.

2.7 kg (6 lb) green tomatoes	2 kg (4½ lb) sugar
rind and juice of 2 lemons	40 g (1½ oz) root ginger
	100 g (4 oz) candied peel

MAKES 3.6 kg (8 lb)

Stalk, wash and very finely slice the tomatoes. Put into a bowl with the lemon rind and juice. Cover with the sugar and leave for 24 hours.

Tie the root ginger in a muslin bag. Finely slice the candied peel. Put the tomato and sugar mixture into a preserving pan with the ginger. Bring to the boil and simmer for about 30 minutes until tender.

When quite thick, remove the ginger and stir in the candied peel. Bring to the boil and boil rapidly for about 10 minutes, stirring occasionally, or until setting point is reached.

Pot the marmalade in warm, clean jars. Cover and seal immediately.

Five Fruit Shred

This is a popular marmalade which you can make at any time of the year, a really useful standby on the larder shelf. It also makes a perfect gift when attractively potted and labelled.

2 oranges	2 large apples
1 grapefruit	2 large pears
1 lemon	1.4 kg (3 lb) sugar
1.7 litres (3 pints) water	

MAKES 2.3 kg (5 lb)

Wash and peel the citrus fruits. Cut off the pith. Shred the rind finely, either with a sharp knife or in a food processor. Chop the flesh coarsely and tie the pith and pips in a muslin bag.

Put the pip bag in a bowl with 300 ml (½ pint) of the water, the shredded peel, chopped fruit and remaining 1.4 litres (2½ pints) water. Soak for 24 hours.

Wash, peel and dice the apples and pears. Put the citrus fruit mixture into a preserving pan, with the apples and pears. Simmer for about 1¼ hours until well reduced, then remove the muslin bag.

Add the sugar and stir over a gentle heat until dissolved. Bring to the boil and boil rapidly for about 10 minutes to setting point. Pot the marmalade in warm, clean jars. Cover and seal immediately.

FIVE FRUIT SHRED (above)

Grapefruit and Pineapple Shred

These two fruits are the perfect counterfoil for each other – a bitter-sweet combination which makes an unusual and original marmalade. I love to make this for Christmas time as something a little bit different.

2 large grapefruit	1×400 g (14 oz) can
2 lemons	crushed pineapple, in
1.25 ml (¼ tsp)	natural juice
bicarbonate of soda	1.8 kg (4 lb) sugar
450 ml (¾ pint) water	

MAKES 2.7 kg (6 lb)

Wash the grapefruit and lemons and remove the rind, cutting off and reserving the white pith. Very finely slice the rind with a sharp knife or in a food processor. Put the rind into a preserving pan with the bicarbonate of soda and water. Cover and simmer for 10 minutes. Drain.

Meanwhile, cut up the fruit pulp, keeping as much of the juices as possible. Tie the pips and pith in a muslin bag. Put the bag of pips into the cleaned preserving pan with the fruit pulp and pineapple. Cover and simmer for 15 minutes.

Add the softened rinds and the sugar. Stir over a gentle heat until the sugar has dissolved. Bring to the boil and boil rapidly for about 10 minutes, stirring occasionally, or until setting point is reached.

Pot the marmalade into warm, clean jars. Cover and seal immediately.

Chunky Apricot and Lemon Marmalade

The individual, delicate taste of apricots makes a lovely marmalade combined with lemons; so when apricots are in plentiful supply in high summer, I often make this recipe.

450 g (1 lb) apricots	1.7 litres (3 pints) water
450 g (1 lb) lemons	1.4 kg (3 lb) sugar

MAKES 2.3 kg (5 lb)

Wash, stone and coarsely chop the apricots. Wash and slice the lemons. Put apricots into a preserving pan with the water and lemon slices. Leave to stand overnight.

Simmer for about 1 hour until very soft. Add the sugar and stir over a medium heat until dissolved. Bring to the boil and boil rapidly for about 10 minutes, stirring occasionally, or until setting point is reached.

Pot the marmalade in warm, clean jars. Cover and seal while still hot.

Chunky Melon Marmalade

Melon takes on a beautiful translucency and texture when it is cooked in syrup, and this lightly set, lemony marmalade adds a touch of style to any breakfast table.

450 g (1 lb) lemons
450 g (1 lb) melon, weight when diced
150 ml (¼ pint) water
pinch of bicarbonate of soda

1.4 kg (3 lb) sugar
225 ml (8 fl oz) pectin

MAKES 2.3 kg (5 lb)

Wash and peel the lemons. Halve and squeeze the juice. Remove the pith and slice the rind coarsely with a sharp knife, or in a mincer or food processor. Dice the melon flesh.

Put the rind into a preserving pan with the water, lemon juice and bicarbonate of soda. Cover and simmer for 10 minutes. Add the melon and simmer for about 10 minutes until tender and transparent.

Add the sugar and stir over a gentle heat until dissolved. Bring to the boil and boil rapidly for 5 minutes. Remove from the heat and stir in the pectin.

Cool a little, skim if necessary and stir once again. Pot the marmalade in warm, clean jars. Cover and seal.

Lemon and Ginger Jelly Marmalade

There are not sufficient adjectives good enough for this marmalade! It is one of my greatest favourites because I love ginger and here, in combination with lemon jelly, it has a quite exquisite taste.

700 g (1½ lb) lemons
1.7 litres (3 pints) water
50 g (2 oz) root ginger

225 g (8 oz) crystallised ginger
900 g (2 lb) sugar

MAKES 2.3 kg (5 lb)

Wash and cut the lemons in quarters. Cut the pith off the rind and reserve it. Cut the rind into fine shreds with a sharp knife or in a mincer or food processor. Put the rind in a large bowl. Cut the fruit finely, reserving the pips. Add the fruit to the bowl and cover with 1.4 litres (2½ pints) of the water. Soak the pips and pith separately in the remaining water for 6 hours.

Tie the root ginger in a muslin bag. Finely chop the crystallised ginger. Strain the water from the pips and pith into a preserving pan and add the bag of ginger. Put in the fruit and rind with its soaking water. Bring to the boil, cover and simmer for 30–40 minutes. Remove the bag and strain the lemon mixture through a jelly bag for 2 hours.

Add the sugar and crystallised ginger. Stir over a low heat until the sugar has dissolved. Bring to the boil and boil rapidly for about 10 minutes, stirring occasionally, or until setting point is reached.

Pot the marmalade in warm, clean jars. Cover and seal.

Lime Marmalade

Now that fresh limes are so much more readily available, it makes sense to make one's own lime marmalade because the home-made variety is so much better than even the best brand name. The colour of this marmalade is the loveliest of greens, an aristocrat amongst marmalades.

450 g (1 lb) ripe limes
750 ml (1¼ pints) water

700 g (1½ lb) sugar

MAKES 1–1.4 kg (2–3 lb)

Wash and thinly pare the limes. Very finely slice the rind. Halve the limes and squeeze the juice. Tie the pips in a muslin bag. Chop the rest of the pulp and tie in a separate muslin bag.

Put the rind, juice, bag of pips, bag of pulp and water into a preserving pan. Bring to the boil and simmer for 1 hour.

Remove the bags. Add the sugar and stir over a gentle heat until dissolved. Bring to the boil and boil rapidly for about 10 minutes, stirring occasionally, or until setting point is reached.

Pot the marmalade in warm, clean jars. Cover and seal immediately.

Tangerine Jelly Marmalade

The disappearance of the tangerine in favour of the satsuma is a pity, I think – I used to love them as a child, and the name is so pretty, too! However, if you cannot obtain tangerines, satsumas make a very good substitute in this beautiful, clear, bright orange marmalade.

1.4 kg (3 lb) tangerines
1.1 litres (2 pints) water
juice of 3 lemons

2.3 kg (5 lb) sugar
225 ml (8 fl oz) pectin

MAKES 3.6 kg (8 lb)

Wash the tangerines. Put into a preserving pan with the water. Cover and simmer for 20–25 minutes. Remove the fruit with a slotted spoon and leave to cool.

Skin the fruit and finely shred the rind. Reserve the pips and coarse tissue and tie these in a muslin bag. Add the bag to the liquid in the pan and boil hard for 5 minutes. Remove the bag of pips and put the fruit and lemon juice into the pan. Simmer for 10 minutes. Strain through a jelly bag overnight.

Return the juice to the cleaned preserving pan. Bring to the boil and boil for a few minutes. Add the sugar and stir over a low heat until dissolved. Add the sliced peel and boil hard for 15 minutes. Remove from the heat and stir in the pectin.

Pot the marmalade in warm, clean jars. Cover and seal immediately.

LIME MARMALADE (left) AND CHUNKY ORANGE HONEY MARMALADE (page 54)

Peach and Pineapple Marmalade

I had never used dried peaches in marmalade before I tried this recipe, and I was astonished at the result. It is almost like a Seville marmalade – lovely and sharp, a beautiful dark orange, with the occasional surprise of a chunk of pineapple to tease the palate.

900 g (2 lb) dried peaches
1×450 g (1 lb) can
   pineapple chunks

grated rind and juice of
   2 lemons
1.8 kg (4 lb) sugar

MAKES 2.7 kg (6 lb)

Rinse and cover the dried peaches with warm water and soak overnight. Put into a preserving pan with the soaking water. Simmer gently for about 20 minutes until tender.

Drain the pineapple chunks and cut each one in half. Remove the peaches from the pan with a slotted spoon, cool slightly, then roughly chop. Return to the pan with the lemon rind and juice, pineapple chunks and sugar. Stir over a gentle heat until the sugar has dissolved. Bring to the boil and boil rapidly for about 10 minutes, stirring occasionally, or until setting point is reached.

Pot the marmalade in warm, clean jars. Cover and seal immediately.

Chunky Fig Marmalade

The combination of dried figs with ginger and lemon is exquisite, and provides a really gastronomic marmalade. As well as being delicious at breakfast time, it makes a very special addition to cream cheese and custards for desserts with a difference.

450 g (1 lb) dried figs
225 g (8 oz) sugar
50 g (2 oz) preserved stem
   ginger

grated rind and juice of 1
   lemon
10 ml (2 tsp) ground
   ginger

MAKES 900 g (2 lb)

Wash and chop the figs. Soak in water to cover overnight. Put the figs and soaking water into a preserving pan and simmer for 10–15 minutes until tender.

Add the sugar and stir over a gentle heat until dissolved. Chop the stem ginger. Add the lemon rind and juice, stem ginger and ground ginger to the pan, stirring well. Bring to the boil and boil rapidly for about 10 minutes, stirring occasionally, or until setting point is reached.

Pot the marmalade in warm, clean jars. Cover and seal.

Tomato and Lemon Shred

This very unusual combination of ingredients makes a delicious marmalade with which I like to surprise guests when they come to stay. A distinguished addition to everyone's larder shelf.

1.8 kg (4 lb) firm ripe tomatoes	3 lemons
100 g (4 oz) crystallised ginger	1.6 kg (3½ lb) sugar
	MAKES 2.3–2.7 kg (5–6 lb)

Pour boiling water over the tomatoes and skin them, then thinly slice. Cut the ginger into thin shreds. Wash and quarter the lemons, then cut into very thin slices. Tie the pips in a muslin bag.

Put the tomatoes into a preserving pan with the lemon, bag of pips, ginger and sugar. Add water to cover. Stand the pan over a very low heat on an asbestos mat to prevent burning. Stir until the sugar has dissolved.

Bring to the boil, then simmer very gently for up to 2 hours until thickened and setting point is reached.

Pot the marmalade in warm, clean jars. Cover and seal immediately.

Dried Apricot and Ginger Marmalade

For anyone who loves apricots and ginger as much as I do, this is THE perfect marmalade. The sharpness of the dried fruit is balanced by the sweet spiciness of the preserved ginger.

450 g (1 lb) dried apricots	5 cm (2 inches) root ginger
1.7 litres (3 pints) water	1.4 kg (3 lb) sugar
100 g (4 oz) preserved ginger	
	MAKES 2.3 kg (5 lb)

Rinse and chop the apricots into small pieces. Put into a bowl, cover with the water and soak for 24 hours.

Cut the preserved ginger into tiny strips. Transfer the fruit to a preserving pan and add the preserved ginger. Tie the root ginger in a muslin bag and add to the pan. Bring slowly to the boil, then simmer for 40 minutes.

Add the sugar and stir over a low heat until dissolved. Bring to the boil and boil rapidly for about 10 minutes, stirring occasionally, or until setting point is reached. Remove the bag.

Pot the marmalade in warm, clean jars. Cover and seal while still hot.

Cherry Marmalade

This marmalade was made for Queen Henrietta Maria, as recorded by her Chancellor and friend, Sir Kenelme Digby in his book of 1669, 'The Closet of Sir Kenelme Digby, Kt. Opened'. Strictly speaking a marmalade is a jam made with citrus fruits, but this one qualifies as such because of its beautifully acidic quality, a sharpness which is gorgeous on breakfast toast, scones and pancakes.

225 g (8 oz) raspberries
1.4 kg (3 lb) cherries
225 g (8 oz) redcurrants

900 g (2 lb) sugar
juice of 1 lemon

MAKES 1.8 kg (4 lb)

Hull and rinse the raspberries. Wash and stone the cherries. Rinse the redcurrants.

Put the raspberries and redcurrants into separate saucepans with water to cover. Bring each to the boil, cover and simmer for 10 minutes. Allow to cool in the pan. When cold, strain off through a sieve.

Put the cherries into a preserving pan with the fruit juices, sugar and lemon juice. Stir over a gentle heat until the sugar has dissolved. Bring to the boil and simmer for about 10 minutes, skimming occasionally, until setting point is reached.

Pot the marmalade in warm, clean jars. Cover and seal immediately.

Chunky Orange Honey Marmalade

This unconventional marmalade is based on one from a very old edition of Mrs Beeton, and is an interesting variation on the theme. The final marmalade is quite dry, rather like a paste of chunky peel sweetened with honey and softened in the cooking. It is well worth making for its individuality, but it has a short shelf life so it must be eaten within three weeks.

Seville oranges
clear honey

Wash and peel the oranges. Put the rinds into a preserving pan with water to cover. Simmer for about 1½ hours until tender. Drain the peel, reserving the cooking liquid, and allow to cool.

Meanwhile, chop the fruit pulp and tie the pips in a muslin bag. Chop the cooled rinds. Add the rinds to the fruit pulp.

Weigh the fruit into the cleaned preserving pan. To every 450 g (1 lb) fruit, add 60 ml (4 tbsp) honey and 300 ml (½ pint) of the reserved cooking liquid. Add the bag of pips and simmer for 30 minutes until reduced and thickened.

Pot the marmalade in warm, clean jars and cover. Allow to cool completely before sealing.

Oxford Marmalade

This world-famous marmalade well deserves its reputation: its deep orange colour is memorable and its uniquely strong flavour quite unforgettable. It is part and parcel of a good British breakfast!

1.5 kg (3 lb) Seville oranges	3 kg (6 lb) sugar
3.6 litres (6 pints) water	MAKES 5 kg (10 lb)

Wash and peel the oranges. Cut the peel into strips and the fruit into small pieces, reserving the pips. Put the pips into a small bowl. Put the strips of peel and chopped flesh into a large bowl. Bring the water to the boil and pour 600 ml (1 pint) over the pips and the remainder over the orange peel and flesh. Cover and leave for several hours or overnight.

Lift the pips out of the water with a slotted spoon and put them in a nylon sieve. Pour the water the pips were soaking in over the pips into the large bowl. Repeat the process, using water from the large bowl. Discard the pips.

Boil the peel, flesh and water for about 2 hours or until the peel is very soft – the longer this mixture boils the darker the marmalade will be. When the peel is quite soft, remove the pan from the heat and add the sugar, stirring until it has dissolved. Boil very gently until the marmalade is as dark as you like it then boil rapidly for about 15 minutes to setting point. Take the pan off the heat and remove any scum with a slotted spoon. Leave to stand for 15 minutes, then stir to distribute the peel. Pot the marmalade in warm, clean jars. Cover and seal immediately.

Windfall Marmalade

The annual crop from the apple tree in my garden is often more than my family can eat fresh, so this recipe has become an established part of our autumn harvesting. It makes a marmalade with a difference – lemon and grapefruit peel in a sumptuous apple base.

1 kg (2 lb) windfall apples	3 litres (5 pints) water
2 grapefruit	2.5 kg (5 lb) sugar
4 lemons	MAKES ABOUT 4.5 kg (9 lb)

Peel, core and chop the apples, reserving the cores and peel. Wash and pare the rinds from the grapefruit and lemons as thinly as possible, using a sharp knife or potato peeler, and shred the rind finely. Remove the pith from the fruits and roughly chop the flesh, removing and reserving any pips. Tie the citrus pith, pips, apple peel and cores in a piece of muslin. Put all the fruit in a preserving pan with the shredded rind, water and muslin bag. Bring to the boil, then simmer gently for about 2½ hours until the peel is soft and the contents of the pan reduced by half.

Remove the muslin bag, squeezing well and allowing the juice to run back into the pan. Add the sugar, stir until it has dissolved, then boil rapidly for 15–20 minutes to setting point. Take the pan off the heat and remove any scum with a slotted spoon. Leave to stand for 15 minutes, then stir to distribute the peel before potting into warm, clean jars. Cover and seal immediately.

Fruit Cheeses, Curds and Butters

FRUIT CHEESES and butters are an ideal way of using up fruit in a time of glut, and also of not wasting the fruit pulp left behind in the jelly bag after making jellies. 'Cheeses' are so called because, cooked as they are to a stiff consistency, they can be cut up into wedges like their dairy namesakes, and served as a dessert or as accompaniments to a wide variety of foods. Butters are of a softer consistency and are usually served as a spread as they contain less sugar and do not store for so long. Curds, which contain butter and eggs in addition to sugar and fruit, have a short shelf life and are not made for storage. Refrigerate and eat as fresh as possible.

◆ SUITABLE FRUITS ◆

Gooseberries, cherries, blackcurrants, quinces, wild plums, apples, apricots, crab apples, blackberries, raisins, lemons, oranges.

BASIC METHODS FOR CHEESE ◆ MAKING ◆

Using the pulp left from making jellies
Remove the fruit pulp from the jelly bag and add enough water to liquidise it to a purée in a blender. Sieve to separate the pulp from the pips and skin. To every 1 pint (600 ml) pulp, add 450 g (1 lb) sugar. Heat the mixture gently until the sugar has dissolved. Continue the cooking as below.

Using fresh fruit
Chop the fruit as necessary and put into a pan with water to just cover. Simmer until very tender. Sieve to separate the pulp from the pips and skin. To every 450 g (1 lb) pulp, add 450 g (1 lb) sugar. Stir until the sugar has dissolved. Add the required spices if any, then simmer gently, stirring occasionally to prevent burning, until a clean line is left when you draw a spoon across it. Grease a mould or jars with glycerine and pour in the cheese to set. Cover and seal. Store in a cool, dark, dry place.

BASIC METHOD FOR CURD ◆ MAKING ◆

A curd is made rather like a cheese or butter but with the extra addition of eggs and butter. To prevent overheating and curdling, use a double boiler, or a bowl over a saucepan of simmering water, for this stage of the cooking. This lets the eggs heat to a solid set without separating and scrambling.

BASIC METHOD FOR
→ BUTTER MAKING ←

The initial cooking is the same as for cheeses, but add 350 g (12 oz) sugar to every 450 g (1 lb) fruit pulp. Stir until the sugar has dissolved. Add the spices indicated in the recipe and cook gently until a thick, creamy consistency is reached. Pack into jars and cover with airtight covers. Immerse the jars in a pan of hot water and boil for 5 minutes. Remove the jars from the water and cool. Store in a cool, dark, dry place.

SERVING IDEAS FOR CHEESES,
→ CURDS AND BUTTERS ←

Cheeses, curds and butters can be served in much the same way as jellies. They go well with cold meats, with a bread and cheese lunch, and can be delicious folded into natural yogurt to flavour and sweeten it. They can be used like jams on bread, toast and scones, or in puddings that would normally use jams. You can serve cheeses as a cold dessert in their own right, with custard or cream, and they are a useful filling for sandwiches, tarts and flans. Butters and curds add a delicious touch to dessert pancakes and a wide variety of hot puddings.

→ STORING ←

Pot cheeses in moulds or jars greased with a little glycerine so that they are easy to turn out when required. While storing, cover with waxed paper and an airtight top. Butters and curds should be stored in clean jars with waxed discs and airtight covers. Store all these preserves in a cool, dark, dry place.

Orange Curd Special

This variation on a theme makes a surprisingly different curd from the lemon one. It is sweeter and less sharp in taste, and has the addition of candied orange peel which makes this curd utterly mouthwatering. Its glowing orange colour looks gorgeous on the tea-table, so with hungry folk around it never lasts for long.

50 g (2 oz) butter	225 g (8 oz) sugar
2 oranges	4 eggs
1 lemon	
50 g (2 oz) candied orange peel	MAKES 700 g (1½ lb)

Put the butter into a bowl and stand it in a pan of hot water until melted or use a double boiler. Wash and finely grate the rinds of the oranges and lemon. Cut the fruit in half and squeeze the juice. Finely chop the candied peel.

Stir the rinds, juice, candied peel and sugar into the butter and stir until the sugar has dissolved. Beat the eggs thoroughly and gradually add to the fruit mixture, stirring continuously. Simmer gently for 5–10 minutes, stirring, until the mixture thickens enough to coat the back of a wooden spoon.

Pot the curd in warm, clean jars. Cover and seal. Store in a cool place, preferably the refrigerator.

Lemon Curd

I love the way that the fresh sharpness of the lemon lifts the rich egg and butter mixture out of blandness, and the smooth thick texture of this curd is irresistible. Lemon curd has so many delicious uses – it is as good on fresh bread and scones as in pastry tarts, or as a filling for crêpes.

6 eggs	450 g (1 lb) sugar
grated rind of 3 lemons	
225 g (8 oz) butter	MAKES 900 g (2 lb)

Separate two of the eggs and set aside the whites to use for other purposes. Beat the four eggs and two extra yolks thoroughly. Squeeze the juices from two of the lemons.

Melt the butter in a bowl over a pan of boiling water, or in a double boiler, and stir in the sugar. When the sugar is warmed through, add the beaten eggs. Stir in the lemon rind and juice. Continue to stir for 5–10 minutes until the curd thickens, taking care that the mixture does not overheat or boil.

Pot the lemon curd in warm, clean jars. Cover and seal. When cold, store in the refrigerator.

ORANGE CURD SPECIAL (above)

Elderberry Curd

To my mind the taste of elderberries is as good as that of blackcurrants, and that is praise indeed for this most underestimated of our wild fruits. In a good year, when they are prolific and succulent, it is well worth making this recipe and serving it as an accompaniment to ice cream or sorbet. Or try folding the elderberry curd into yogurt to make a simple but memorable dessert.

450 g (1 lb) elderberries	350 g (12 oz) sugar
100 g (4 oz) butter	4 eggs

MAKES 1.4 kg (3 lb)

Wash the berries. Put into a preserving pan with a little water. Simmer for 10–15 minutes until soft. Sieve to separate the pulp from the pips.

Put the purée into a bowl with the butter and sugar. Place the bowl over a pan of simmering water until the sugar has dissolved, stirring well. Alternatively, use a double boiler.

Beat the eggs, add to the fruit purée and stir over the hot water for 5–10 minutes until the mixture thickens.

Pot the curd in warm, clean jars. Cover and seal. Store in a cool place, preferably the refrigerator.

Plum Gumbo

A traditional American recipe, this interesting mixture of plums, oranges and raisins makes a thick and sumptuous spread for tea-time treats. Potted up with pretty labels and a fabric circle to cover the jar, it makes an original gift, too.

1.4 kg (3 lb) plums	1.4 kg (3 lb) sugar
2 oranges	450 g (1 lb) seedless
450 ml (¾ pint) water	raisins

MAKES 2.7 kg (6 lb)

Wash, halve and stone the plums. Wash, peel and finely slice the oranges. Put the plums into a preserving pan with the water. Simmer for 10–15 minutes until tender and quite pulpy.

Sieve the plums and return to the cleaned preserving pan with the orange slices, sugar and raisins. Stir over a low heat until the sugar has dissolved, then continue cooking for 5–10 minutes, stirring occasionally, until the mixture is thick.

Pot the gumbo in warm, clean jars. Cover and seal.

Pear Carnival Cheese

This brightly coloured preserve deserves its carnival description – it is a mixture of red, green, orange and yellow, and full of appetising tastes and textures. This cheese is one of the best preserves on freshly baked bread, and makes an unbeatable filling for an almond pastry case, served with whipped cream.

1.4 kg (3 lb) pears	**sugar**
1×400 g (14 oz) can pineapple chunks, drained	**150 ml (¼ pint) bottle maraschino cherries**
grated rind and juice of 1 orange	MAKES 1.8 kg (4 lb)

Wash, peel and core the pears. Cut the flesh into 1 cm (½ inch) cubes. Add the pineapple and orange rind and juice.

Weigh the fruits into a bowl. To every 450 g (1 lb) fruit, add 350 g (12 oz) sugar, sprinkling it over the fruits. Leave to stand overnight.

Transfer the mixture to a preserving pan and simmer gently for 5–10 minutes, stirring frequently, until the mixture thickens. Cut the cherries in half and stir into the fruit.

Pot the cheese in warm, clean wide-necked jars. Cover and seal. Store in a cool, dark place.

Raisin Cheese

This delectable cheese makes one of the most unexpectedly original additions to the store cupboard. It is a delicious variation on a kind of mincemeat theme: gorgeous in little light pastry cases or vol-au-vents, just warmed through, or as a filling for dessert crêpes.

450 g (1 lb) seedless raisins	**10 ml (2 tsp) ground cloves**
225 g (8 oz) sugar	**100 g (4 oz) candied peel**
10 ml (2 tsp) ground cinnamon	MAKES 900 g (2 lb)

Put the raisins into a preserving pan with water to cover, the sugar and spices. Simmer gently for 30 minutes, stirring continuously, until thick and stiff. Cool a little, then stir in the candied peel.

Pot the cheese in small, warm, clean jars. Store in a dark, dry place.

Blackberry Cheese

Small wonder that hordes of people have eagerly gathered the blackberry harvest over the centuries. It is the finest and, happily, one of the most prolific of our wild fruits, and has provided us with many classic pies and puddings, jams and jellies. This smooth, pipless cheese is a beautiful dark purplish-red in colour, and is delicious served with thick set yogurt or with ice cream.

900 g (2 lb) blackberries
300 ml (½ pint) water

MAKES 1.4 kg (3 lb)

Rinse the blackberries. Put into a preserving pan with the water. Cover and simmer for about 15–20 minutes until very soft. Rub the blackberries through a sieve. Return the pulp to the pan and continue cooking for 5–10 minutes to reduce the liquid content.

Measure the pulp into the cleaned preserving pan. To every 600 ml (1 pint) pulp, add 450 g (1 lb) sugar. Stir over a low heat until the sugar has dissolved. Simmer gently for 10–15 minutes until the mixture is thick.

Grease warm, clean jars with a little glycerine. Pot the cheese in the jars. Cover and seal.

Cherry Cheese

If you arm yourself with one of those great little gadgets, a stoner, which takes the stones out of small fruits cleanly and quickly, the time and effort taken to make this recipe will be greatly reduced. Ripe cherries are always a treat in high summer, so this is a luxury on the larder shelf when they are long out of season.

cherries
sugar

Wash and stone the cherries, removing the stalks, working over a preserving pan so that no juice is wasted, and using a stoner for this operation. Put into a preserving pan with a little water and simmer very gently until the cherries are soft. Liquidise to a purée and then pass through a sieve to separate the pulp from the skins.

Weigh the pulp into the cleaned preserving pan. Bring to the boil and simmer for 5–10 minutes until a dry paste. To every 450 g (1 lb) fruit, add 450 g (1 lb) sugar. Stir over a low heat until the sugar has dissolved, then stir continuously until a smooth, dry paste is obtained.

Grease small, warm, clean jars with a little glycerine. Pot the cheese into the prepared jars. Cover and seal.

BLACKBERRY CHEESE (above)

Cranberry Cheese

I love to serve this at Christmas instead of the traditional jelly, just for a change. It is thick and soft in texture, yet sharp and clean in taste, and takes a lot of beating as an accompaniment to roast turkey.

750 g (1½ lb) cranberries, washed	**750 g (1½ lb) sugar**
900 ml (1½ pints) water	MAKES ABOUT 1 kg (2 lb)

Put the cranberries in a saucepan with the water, bring to the boil then simmer gently for about 1 hour, or until the fruit is tender. Using a wooden spoon, press the fruit pulp through a nylon sieve. Return the purée to a clean pan, add the sugar and heat gently, stirring, until the sugar has dissolved. Bring to the boil and boil rapidly for about 30 minutes until the mixture is so thick the spoon leaves a clean line through the mixture when drawn across the bottom of the pan.

Grease warm, clean jars with a little glycerine. Pot the cheese in the jars. Cover and seal.

Gooseberry Curd

All the curds are delicious, but for me there is something special about this one. The summery flavour of gooseberries in this creamy mixture makes it utterly delicious on toast or on freshly baked scones, and I also like to serve it rolled up in crêpes, with a little cream, as a dessert.

1.5 kg (3 lb) green gooseberries	**100 g (4 oz) butter**
450 ml (¾ pint) water	**4 eggs, lightly beaten**
750 g (1½ lb) caster sugar	MAKES 2 kg (4 lb)

Top, tail and wash the gooseberries. Put them with the water in a saucepan and simmer gently for 20 minutes, or until tender. Using a wooden spoon, press the gooseberry pulp through a nylon sieve into the top of a double saucepan or a bowl standing over a pan of simmering water. Add the sugar, butter and eggs. Heat gently, stirring, for about 20 minutes until the sugar has dissolved and the mixture thickens, taking care that the mixture does not overheat or boil.

Strain, then pot in small, warm, clean jars. Cover and seal. When cold, store in the refrigerator.

Crunchy Harvest Butter

A delectable hint of walnuts highlights both the flavour and the texture of the apple purée that forms the basis of this recipe. The added crunch of natural wheatgerm is quite unusual, and if you choose to make the butter with crab apples their slightly sharper taste combines particularly well with the overall nutty taste.

1.5 kg (3 lb) cooking apples, windfalls or crab apples about 1 litre (1¾ pints) water sugar	50 g (2 oz) walnuts, finely chopped 45 ml (3 tbsp) crunchy natural wheatgerm MAKES 1.5 kg (3 lb)

Wash and chop the apples. Put into a saucepan, cover with water, bring to the boil and simmer gently for about 1 hour until really soft and pulpy. Using a wooden spoon, press the apple pulp through a nylon sieve and measure the purée. Return the purée to the pan and add 375 g (12 oz) sugar for each 600 ml (1 pint) purée. Heat gently, stirring, until the sugar has dissolved, then bring to the boil and boil for 30–45 minutes, stirring frequently, until the mixture is thick and like jam in consistency. Stir in the walnuts and wheatgerm. Pot the butter in warm, clean jars and cover with airtight tops. Immerse in a pan of hot water and boil for 5 minutes. Remove the jars from the water and cool. Store in a dark, dry, cool place.

Apricot and Orange Butter

The two fruity flavours of apricot and orange are beautifully balanced in this recipe, and complement each other perfectly. It makes a delicious accompaniment to roast chicken, as well as being irresistible on fresh granary toast.

1.5 kg (3 lb) fresh apricots grated rind and juice of 2 oranges	about 450 ml (¾ pint) water sugar MAKES ABOUT 1.5 kg (3 lb)

Skin and stone the apricots. Put them with the orange rind and juice in a pan and add just enough water to cover. Simmer gently for about 45 minutes until the fruit is soft and pulpy. Press the fruit through a sieve. Measure the purée and return it to the pan with 375 g (12 oz) sugar for each 600 ml (1 pint) purée. Heat gently, stirring, until the sugar has dissolved, then bring to the boil and boil for 30–40 minutes, stirring frequently, until the mixture is thick and like jam in consistency. Pot the butter in warm, clean jars and cover with airtight tops. Immerse in a pan of hot water and boil for 5 minutes. Remove the jars from the water and cool. Store in a dark, dry, cool place.

Crab Apple Butter

This is based on an old traditional country recipe of the 18th century; a time when the housewife made the most of the wild harvest every autumn, and when these fruits were cherished for their food value as well as their delicious flavours. This spicy butter goes particularly well with roast meat or chicken, either hot or as part of a cold table.

1.4 kg (3 lb) crab apples	5 cm (2 inch) stick
600 ml (1 pint) cider	cinnamon
600 ml (1 pint) water	2.5 ml (½ tsp) cloves
sugar	
	MAKES 2.3 kg (5 lb)

Wash and cut the crab apples into quarters. Put in a preserving pan with the cider and water. Simmer for 15–20 minutes until soft and pulpy. Press the fruit through a sieve.

Weigh the pulp into the cleaned preserving pan. To every 450 g (1 lb) pulp, add 350 g (12 oz) sugar. Stir over a low heat until the sugar has dissolved. Tie the spices in a muslin bag and add to the pan. Bring to the boil, stirring frequently, and simmer for 5–10 minutes until the mixture is a thick, creamy consistency.

Pot the butter in warm, clean jars and cover with airtight tops. Immerse in a pan of hot water and boil for 5 minutes. Remove the jars from the water and cool. Store in a dark, dry, cool place.

Wild Plum Butter

Returning home from a chilly autumn ramble armed with a little basket full of wild plums is one of the many delights of the annual hedgerow harvest. This way of using them is one of the most delightful, as their sharp and distinctive flavour is an excellent foil for the smooth, slightly spiced butter.

wild plums (damsons or bullaces)	sugar
whole skinned almonds	ground allspice to taste

Wash and pick the stalks off the plums. Chop a few almonds. Put the plums into a preserving pan with a little water. Simmer for 10–15 minutes until soft, stirring occasionally. Press the plums through a coarse sieve.

Measure the sieved fruit into the cleaned preserving pan. To every 450 g (1 lb) pulp, add 350 g (12 oz) sugar. Stir over a gentle heat until the sugar has dissolved. Add the allspice to taste and the chopped almonds. Simmer gently for 5–10 minutes until the mixture is a smooth, buttery consistency.

Pot the butter in warm, clean jars and cover with airtight tops. Immerse in a pan of hot water and boil for 5 minutes. Remove the jars from the water and cool. Store in a dark, dry, cool place.

Special Conserves

CONSERVES have a special quality all their own – a touch of luxury, of originality, to which can be added their good looks. The way that the whole fruits are preserved in syrup makes the jars, glistening with seductive goodies, look really mouthwatering. It is worth saving extra-large jars for this operation, or even buying them specially, to show the conserves off to their best advantage. It is well worth experimenting with the wide range of tropical fruits that are available to add an extravagant touch to the larder shelf.

BEST FRUITS FOR MAKING CONSERVES

Since conserves are made rather as luxury items, it is best to choose fruits that are going to look good in the jars: all the soft summer fruits lend themselves well to conserves – strawberries, raspberries, gooseberries, blackcurrants, red and white currants, cranberries – and, later on in the year, blackberries. Tiny kumquats look gorgeous preserved whole, so do chunks of pineapple and quartered nectarines. Apricots, whether dried or fresh, take on a golden glow when preserved in syrup, and make some of the very best conserves.

STORING

These special conserves are not made for long storage. The only preservatives they contain are sugar and a little alcohol or vinegar, so their shelf life is fairly short. It is best to eat them within six weeks, even sooner if they show any signs of mould. Keep conserves in as cool a place as possible – if you have room to keep them in the refrigerator, they will keep for slightly longer.

STERILISING JARS

Some people like to sterilise their jars before filling them with preserves, and this is quite simply done. You can buy sterilising tablets from some chemists, with which you make a solution in water. Following the precise instructions on the packet, immerse the clean jars into the solution, then drain and dry them before use. There is a school of thought, however, that sterilisation tends to add a slight but nonetheless offensive taste to the preserve, and that just to wash the jars in very hot water is an adequate precaution against marauding bacteria!

JARS

Choose wide-necked, large jars for storing conserves, and if you are making them as gifts you may feel moved to go so far as to buy special ones. There is a variety to choose from, with details like fluting, faceting and beading, and some made with tinted glass. When you fill the jars with your luscious conserves and package them up as gifts, these make extra special presents, home-made with style.

MAKING UP GIFT JARS

One of the prettiest ways of converting a plain glass jar into an attractive looking gift is to cut out a circle of printed fabric 2.5 cm (1 inch) larger in diameter than the top of the jar. Cut it using pinking shears if you can, to give the edge a zig-zag pattern and also to stop it from fraying. Place the fabric circle evenly over the top of the sealed jar, and tie it down with fine cord or very thin ribbon, making a secure knot first and then tying it into a bow.

There are a number of very pretty self-adhesive labels for preserves on the market nowadays, so it is worth hunting around for ones that will look good with the type of fabric you have chosen. Neatly write, in coloured felt-tip pen to match your colour scheme, the name of the preserve, with the date on which it was made. Stick the label on, and you have a handsome gift to give away.

Spiced Green Figs

To my mind, ripe figs are amongst the most sensual of summer fruits, and their richness and soft texture lend themselves beautifully to spicing with cinnamon and cloves. Serve these figs as part of a cold table – they are really delicious with cheeses, salads, and cold meats of all kinds.

1.8 kg (4 lb) ripe figs	600 ml (1 pint) vinegar
2 litres (3½ pints) strong brine (see page 85)	15 g (½ oz) stick cinnamon
900 g (2 lb) sugar	15 g (½ oz) cloves

MAKES 3.2 kg (7 lb)

Wipe the figs. Put into a bowl and pour over the brine. Leave to soak overnight.

Rinse the figs thoroughly in cold water and dry well. Pack into clean jars.

Put the sugar and vinegar in a heavy pan. Stir over a gentle heat until the sugar has dissolved. Tie the spices in a muslin bag and add to the pan. Bring to the boil and simmer for 5 minutes. Remove the spices and boil the vinegar hard for about 5 minutes to reduce.

Pour the boiling vinegar over the figs. Leave until cold. Cover and seal.

Spiced Gooseberries

Gooseberries lend themselves beautifully to savoury treatment, and this spicy conserve makes a lovely addition to a ploughman's lunch or a salad buffet table. Excellent with coleslaw, too.

2.7 kg (6 lb) gooseberries
1.8 kg (4 lb) sugar
300 ml (½ pint) malt
  vinegar

10 ml (2 tsp) ground
  cinnamon
10 ml (2 tsp) allspice
5 ml (1 tsp) ground cloves

MAKES 3.6 kg (8 lb)

Top, tail and wash the gooseberries. Drain and dry them thoroughly.

Place the gooseberries in large jars or dishes and sprinkle over the sugar. Stand the jars in the oven at 170°C (325°F) mark 3 and heat for 1 hour.

Transfer the sweetened gooseberries to an aluminium preserving pan. Stir in the vinegar and spices. Bring to the boil and boil for about 20–30 minutes until very thick.

Pot the conserve in warm, clean jars. Cover and seal.

Spiced Blackberries

Since most blackberry recipes are for sweet preserves, it is rather nice to try a savoury one for a change. These spiced blackberries keep indefinitely and I love to take them on summer picnics or to serve them with a cheese and salad meal. The blackberries retain all their distinctive and delicate flavour, and are excellent just with plain bread and cheese.

900 g (2 lb) blackberries
450 g (1 lb) sugar
300 ml (½ pint) vinegar
5 ml (1 tsp) allspice
  berries

5 ml (1 tsp) cloves
5 ml (1 tsp) ground ginger

MAKES 1.4 kg (3 lb)

Wash and pick over the blackberries. Put the sugar in an aluminium preserving pan with the vinegar and stir over a gentle heat until dissolved.

Put the whole spices in a muslin bag and add to the pan. Simmer for several minutes. Add the blackberries and ginger and poach gently for 10–15 minutes. Remove the bag of spices.

Pack the blackberries into warm, clean jars. Boil the vinegar hard until it turns syrupy. Pour the vinegar over the blackberries. Cover and seal.

Brandied Apricots

*I love to make jars of these as little presents –
the golden glow of apricots set in a glistening
syrup, which is laced with brandy, looks and
tastes quite epicurean. Attractively labelled, and
with a circle of printed fabric over the top of the
jar, they make personal and original gifts.*

900 g (2 lb) fresh apricots
225 g (8 oz) sugar

300 ml (½ pint) brandy

MAKES 900 g (2 lb)

Wipe the apricots and remove the stones as carefully
as possible without injuring the fruit. Put into a large
glass container, such as a kilner jar, sprinkling with
the sugar as you fill. Pour the brandy over the fruit
and tightly cover the jar.

Place the jar in a pan of simmering water and
bring the brandy to simmering, but do not allow it to
boil. Heat at this point for 15–20 minutes.

Carefully remove the fruit with a slotted spoon
and place into small, warm, clean jars. Pour over the
sweetened brandy. Leave until cold. Cover and seal.

Brandy Berries

*I came across this delectable conserve when I
visited my American aunt some time ago and it
has remained in my memory as being quite
outstandingly delicious. Cherries, plums or
peaches can be used instead of cranberries. This
conserve is, of course, a luxury because of its
liberal use of spirits but well worth treating
yourself to!*

**450 g (1 lb) fresh
   cranberries**
450 g (1 lb) sugar
grated rind of 1 orange

**150 ml (¼ pint) Grand
   Marnier and brandy
   mixed**

MAKES 900 g (2 lb)

Wash and dry the cranberries and pick them over.
Put the cranberries, sugar, orange rind and liqueur
and brandy in a large, flat, ovenproof dish and leave
to stand for 30 minutes.

Cover the dish with foil and cook in the oven at
170°C (325°F) mark 3 for 30 minutes. Cool slightly.

Pot the conserve in warm, clean jars. Cover and
seal. Store in a cool place.

BRANDY BERRIES (above)

Holiday Conserve

This luxury mixture of apricots, glacé fruits and nuts, flavoured with orange and lemon, is a real treat which I like to have on hand when it is holiday time. Served with home-made ice cream and brandy-snaps, we never fail to feel festive!

450 g (1 lb) canned apricot halves
225 g (8 oz) mixed glacé fruits
100 g (4 oz) glacé cherries
225 g (8 oz) sugar
1.25 ml (¼ tsp) salt
1.25 ml (¼ tsp) grated nutmeg
grated rind of 1 orange
grated rind of 1 lemon
350 g (12 oz) Brazil nuts or walnuts

MAKES 1.4 kg (3 lb)

Drain the apricots, reserving the syrup, and coarsely chop. Make the syrup up to 450 ml (¾ pint) with water.

Place all the ingredients, except the nuts, in a preserving pan. Bring to the boil, stirring occasionally, and simmer for 25 minutes until thickened.

Finely chop the nuts and stir into the conserve for the last 5 minutes of cooking.

Pot the conserve in warm, clean jars. Cover and seal.

Orange Cranberry Conserve

It has become far easier to buy fresh cranberries in recent years, and this orange-flavoured mixture with raisins and nuts makes a speciality conserve. As well as a treat to have in store, it also makes a lovely gift – a present with a difference.

450 g (1 lb) cranberries
2 oranges
300 ml (½ pint) water
50 g (2 oz) raisins
50 g (2 oz) walnuts
350 g (12 oz) sugar

MAKES 900 g (2 lb)

Wash and pick over the cranberries. Wash, peel and finely slice the oranges, discarding the pips. Cut the slices into quarters.

Put the fruit into a preserving pan with the water. Simmer for about 15–20 minutes until tender.

Add the raisins, walnuts and sugar. Stir over a gentle heat until the sugar has dissolved. Bring to the boil and boil rapidly for about 10 minutes, stirring occasionally, or until setting point is reached.

Pot the conserve in warm, clean jars. Cover immediately and seal when cold.

Preserved Nectarines

I made these as Christmas presents one year and they made a real impact – the friends who received them all wanted the recipe and so here, in all its simplicity, it is.

450 g (1 lb) nectarines	150 ml (¼ pint) peach
450 g (1 lb) sugar	brandy
150 ml (¼ pint) water	
	MAKES 900 g (2 lb)

Wash, halve and stone the nectarines. Put the sugar into a preserving pan with the water and stir over a gentle heat until dissolved. Bring to the boil and boil for 10 minutes to make a syrup.

Place the nectarines in the hot syrup and poach, just below simmering point, for 5 minutes. Leave to cool in the syrup.

Lift out the fruit with a slotted spoon and put into warm, clean jars. Reheat the syrup and boil hard for 5 minutes. Cool a little and stir in the brandy.

Pour the brandy syrup over the nectarines. Leave to cool. Cover and seal when cold. Store in a cool, dry place.

Pear and Pineapple Conserve

The combination of these two fruits, glistening in syrup and slightly translucent, is quite lovely – and it tastes as delicious as it looks. This conserve is fabulous with a sharp-tasting citrus sorbet and ice cream, especially coffee-flavoured.

900 g (2 lb) sugar	900 g (2 lb) pears
600 ml (1 pint) water	1 large pineapple
	MAKES 2.3 kg (5 lb)

Put the sugar into a preserving pan with the water and stir until dissolved. Bring to the boil and simmer for 10 minutes until a fairly thick syrup.

Wash, peel and core the pears, then slice into eight segments each. Remove the skin from the pineapple and cut the flesh into thick slices. Chop each slice into eight triangles.

Place the pineapple pieces in the syrup and poach for 30 minutes, then add the pears for the last 10 minutes of the cooking time.

Lift out the fruit and put into warm, clean jars. Pour over the syrup. Leave to cool. Cover and seal when cold. Store in a cool, dry place.

Orange Mincemeat

This is my very favourite mincemeat recipe, so fruity and fresh, instead of the rather heavy, solid mincemeats that abound. It is good enough to eat out of the jar, but if you can resist doing that, try filling little vol-au-vent cases with the mincemeat and heating them through gently – they are quite scrumptious.

450 g (1 lb) apples	225 g (8 oz) unskinned
2 oranges	whole almonds
2 lemons	100 g (4 oz) ground
450 g (1 lb) currants	almonds
450 g (1 lb) raisins	225 g (8 oz) demerara
225 g (8 oz) sultanas	sugar
225 g (8 oz) candied peel	150 ml (¼ pint) brandy

MAKES 2.7 kg (6 lb)

Wash, peel, core and chop the apples. Wash and pare the rind off the oranges and lemons and shred them finely. Simmer the shredded rind in a saucepan of boiling water for 10 minutes. Drain and cool. Squeeze the juice from the oranges and lemons.

Mix the apples, currants, raisins and sultanas with the fruit juices and put small amounts at a time through a food processor just to break them up a little.

Chop the candied peel. Coarsely chop the whole almonds. Stir the rinds, ground almonds, candied peel, sugar, almonds and brandy into the apple mixture and mix thoroughly.

Pot the mincemeat in clean jars. Cover and seal. Store in a cool, dark, dry place for up to 3 months.

Strawberries in Wine

This is a summer treat with a difference which I love to make when the strawberry season is at its height and I have enough jam on the shelf. Served with a sorbet or ice cream, these strawberries in their delicious wine syrup make a fantastic finale to a meal.

strawberries
sugar
sherry or Madeira

Hull, rinse and dry the strawberries, then weigh them. To every 450 g (1 lb) fruit, use 100 g (4 oz) sugar.

Put the strawberries into jars, sprinkling with the sugar as you fill. When the fruit reaches the neck of the jar, fill it up with sherry or Madeira.

Cover and seal tightly. Store in a cold place, preferably the refrigerator.

STRAWBERRIES IN WINE (above)

Chutneys

A WIDE variety of fruit and vegetables can be used to make chutneys. Traditionally, apples and onions provide the basis, with sultanas, raisins and dates often to be found on the ingredients list. Plums, marrows, gooseberries and tomatoes also make lovely chutneys, and shallots and garlic are often added to give them zest and flavour. Chutneys are frequently laced with hot spices such as chillies, peppercorns and mustard seeds to provide a hot tang.

While most fruit and vegetables are boiled up to produce a thick mixture, there is a range of chutneys which are uncooked, and are served rather like condiments to spice up a meal.

◆ BASIC METHOD ◆

Use fresh fruit or vegetables which are not over-ripe or damaged. Prepare them and put into an aluminium pan (metals such as brass, copper or iron will react with the acid in the vinegar and spoil both the chutney and the pan). If you choose to use a pressure cooker, never fill it more than half full and, generally speaking, cook at 6.8 kg (15 lb) pressure for 10 minutes. When cooking in an open preserving pan, long steady cooking is required for a good chutney, but do not over-boil it. As soon as the mixture thickens to the point where pools of vinegar no longer collect on the surface, the chutney is ready. If sieving is called for, use a hair or nylon sieve, since a metal one will impart an unpleasant taste.

Allow the cooked chutney to cool for a while in the preserving pan before bottling because it tends to shrink quite considerably as it loses heat. Pot in clean jars when tepid, prodding out any air bubbles from the mixture and making sure that the chutney is well packed down. Cover with waxed discs, again ensuring against air bubbles, and put on an outer cellophane disc. Screw down with plastic screw tops – never use metal for chutney as it will rust and corrode. Wipe the jars clean with a damp cloth, then label. Store in a cool, dark, dry place. Some chutneys keep for many years, even up to twenty, and improve greatly with keeping.

◆ HOW TO SERVE ◆

Serve chutneys with hot meals like curries, rice dishes, stews and casseroles. They make a pleasant change to eat with roast chicken or lamb, and certain ones are excellent with fish dishes. Try mixing small amounts of chutney into stuffings to spice them up and sharpen the flavour. A selection of chutneys greatly enhances a cold table – they are excellent with salads and cold meats.

Mango Chutney

The classic accompaniment to an Indian meal of curries and rice, this sweet chutney, with its mouthwatering texture, is well worth making. I love mango chutney with cheese, too, especially a strong blue Stilton or Gorgonzola. With some fresh bread, it makes a perfect meal.

900 g (2 lb) mangoes	600 ml (1 pint) vinegar
50 g (2 oz) salt	450 g (1 lb) sugar
450 g (1 lb) cooking apples	2.5 ml (½ tsp) grated nutmeg
100 g (4 oz) onions	2.5 ml (½ tsp) ground cinnamon
2 limes	
75 g (3 oz) root ginger	100 g (4 oz) stoned raisins

MAKES 1.8 kg (4 lb)

Peel and finely slice the mangoes. Put them into a bowl and sprinkle with the salt. Wash, core and chop the apples. Skin and slice the onions. Wash and slice the limes. Bruise the ginger and tie in a muslin bag.

Put half of the vinegar into an aluminium preserving pan with the sugar and stir over a medium heat until dissolved. Bring to the boil and boil for 5–8 minutes to make a syrup.

Add the rest of the vinegar, the mangoes, spices and onions. Simmer for 10 minutes. Add the remaining ingredients and simmer for a further 40–50 minutes until thick.

Cool, then pack the chutney into clean jars. Cover and seal.

Fig and Nut Chutney

Rich and thick, this exciting combination of fresh figs, dates and nuts makes an exquisite and piquant side dish to accompany plain roast chicken. It is also delicious with lightly spiced rice and a tomato and onion salad.

700 g (1½ lb) fresh figs	75 g (3 oz) seedless raisins
225 g (8 oz) onions	225 g (8 oz) brown sugar
75 g (3 oz) stoned dates	600 ml (1 pint) vinegar
50 g (2 oz) preserved ginger	2.5 ml (½ tsp) salt
175 g (6 oz) hazelnuts	1.25 ml (¼ tsp) cayenne

MAKES 2.3 kg (5 lb)

Wipe and slice the figs. Skin and slice the onions. Chop the dates, ginger, nuts and raisins. Put the sugar in an aluminium preserving pan with the vinegar and stir over a medium heat until dissolved. Bring to the boil and simmer for 10 minutes.

Put the other ingredients into a large bowl and pour over the sweetened vinegar. Leave to stand overnight.

Return the mixture to the pan and bring slowly to the boil. Simmer for 1–2 hours until dark and thick.

Cool, then pack the chutney into clean jars. Cover and seal.

Carrot Chutney

This rather dry, slightly sweet chutney is very versatile. I love to serve it with salads of all kinds at any time of the year. Carrot chutney makes a delicious addition to stuffings, making them a little different. It goes beautifully with cream cheese and cottage cheese, too, adding texture and spice to their blandness.

900 g (2 lb) carrots
175 g (6 oz) brown sugar
100 g (4 oz) sultanas
900 ml (1½ pints) vinegar
10 ml (2 tsp) ground
   ginger

10 ml (2 tsp) mixed spice
12 peppercorns
2 bay leaves

MAKES 1.4 kg (3 lb)

Wash, scrape and coarsely grate the carrots. Put into an aluminium preserving pan with all the other ingredients. Simmer for about 10 minutes until tender and thickened, and the liquid has evaporated.

Cool, skimming occasionally. Pack the chutney into clean jars. Cover and seal.

Apricot and Sultana Chutney

Sweet chutneys provide a delicious finishing touch to cold meats, cheeses and salads. This slightly hot, spicy way of dealing with dried apricots and sultanas is an original and ever popular addition to cold, simple fare.

700 g (1½ lb) dried
   apricots
900 ml (1½ pints) hot
   water
10 large garlic cloves
7.5 cm (3 inch) piece of
   fresh root ginger

300 ml (½ pint) vinegar
450 g (1 lb) sugar
1.25 ml (¼ tsp) salt
1.25 ml (¼ tsp) cayenne
175 g (6 oz) sultanas

MAKES 2.3 kg (5 lb)

Rinse and put the apricots in a bowl with the hot water. Leave to soak for 4 hours.

Chop the garlic. Peel and chop the ginger. Blend the garlic and ginger with a little of the vinegar until smooth. Put the apricots with their soaking water and the ginger and garlic mixture into an aluminium preserving pan with the rest of the vinegar. Add the sugar, salt and cayenne. Bring to the boil and simmer gently for 45 minutes, stirring occasionally to prevent burning.

Add the sultanas and continue cooking until the chutney thickens and begins to turn shiny.

Cool and pack in clean jars. Cover and seal.

APRICOT AND SULTANA CHUTNEY (above)

Grapefruit Chutney

This is one of my firm favourites, because of the lovely sharp flavour of grapefruit and the unexpected crunch of chopped almonds. It is fabulous with an aubergine curry and basmati rice, and is a delicious accompaniment to an avocado and raw mushroom salad.

900 g (2 lb) grapefruit pulp	600 ml (1 pint) vinegar
700 g (1½ lb) granulated sugar	100 g (4 oz) seedless raisins
5 ml (1 tsp) ground cloves	100 g (4 oz) sultanas
5 ml (1 tsp) cayenne	12 almonds
	MAKES 2.3 kg (5 lb)

Discard the pips and pith from the grapefruit pulp. Put the pulp into an aluminium preserving pan with the sugar. Stir over a gentle heat until the sugar has dissolved.

Stir in the ground spices, vinegar, raisins and sultanas. Bring to the boil and simmer gently until soft and thick. Chop the almonds and stir into the chutney towards the end of the cooking time.

Cool, then pack the chutney into clean jars. Cover and seal.

Aubergine Chutney

This recipe comes from India where the word 'chutney' originates – 'chatni', a Hindi word, means a relish of sweet fruits or vegetables with vinegar and spices. Serve this one with a meat or vegetable curry and rice, and it really comes into its own.

900 g (2 lb) aubergines	10 ml (2 tsp) ground ginger
350 g (12 oz) onions	5 ml (1 tsp) salt
450 g (1 lb) cooking apples	550 g (1¼ lb) dark brown sugar
10 ml (2 tsp) pickling spice	MAKES 2.3 kg (5 lb)
300 ml (½ pint) vinegar	

Peel and cut the aubergines into long segments, then into thickish slices. Skin and very finely chop the onions. Wash, core and roughly chop the apples. Tie the pickling spice in a muslin bag.

Put all the ingredients, except the sugar, into an aluminium preserving pan and simmer for 30–40 minutes until tender. Remove the spice bag and add the sugar. Stir over a gentle heat until the sugar has dissolved. Simmer until the chutney becomes thick and lustrous.

Cool, then pack the chutney into clean jars. Cover and seal.

Autumn Chutney

There is nothing quite like the satisfaction to be gained from using up surplus vegetables and fruits at the end of the summer as the evenings close in a little and the air begins to chill. The smell of this lovely mixed chutney always reminds me of those golden, slightly misty days as we prepare for winter.

450 g (1 lb) plums
450 g (1 lb) apples
450 g (1 lb) tomatoes
450 g (1 lb) onions
2 large garlic cloves
450 g (1 lb) sultanas
600 ml (1 pint) vinegar

1.25 ml (¼ tsp) mace
1.25 ml (¼ tsp) ground mixed spice
15 g (½ oz) ground ginger
450 g (1 lb) demerara sugar

MAKES 3.2 kg (7 lb)

Wash, halve and stone the plums. Peel and core the apples. Wash and chop the tomatoes. Skin and slice the onions. Skin and chop the garlic.

Mix the fruit and vegetables together and put into an aluminium preserving pan with all the other ingredients, except the sugar. Simmer for about 30 minutes until tender.

Add the sugar and stir until dissolved. Simmer gently, stirring frequently, until thick.

Cool, then pack the chutney into clean jars. Cover and seal.

Bengal Chutney

A hot chutney to raise the roof of the mouth!
Not for timid tastebuds this one, but for chilli-lovers for whom a hot chutney makes a complete meal of a vindaloo! Keep for 2–3 years before using – it improves greatly with keeping, and the longer the better.

15 large cooking apples	450 g (1 lb) demerara
225 g (8 oz) onions	sugar
100 g (4 oz) garlic	1.7 litres (3 pints) vinegar
2 fresh chillies	50 g (2 oz) mustard seeds
225 g (8 oz) stoned raisins	50 g (2 oz) ground ginger

MAKES 3.6 kg (8 lb)

Wash the apples and bake in the oven at 180°C (350°F) mark 4 for 20–30 minutes until soft. Scoop out the flesh from the skins and remove the pips.

Skin and chop the onions and put into a pan of boiling water with the garlic. Simmer for about 20 minutes until soft.

Wash and slice the chillies. Put the onion and apple pulp into a preserving pan with all the other ingredients. Bring to the boil and simmer for 15–20 minutes.

Pack the chutney into warm, clean jars. Leave to cool. Cover and seal.

Banana and Lychee Chutney

The texture of lychees gives a mouthwatering crunch to this unusual chutney. The flavour of banana provides a distinctive taste, and it makes an elegant companion to a dish of cold chicken.

12 lychees	225 g (8 oz) raisins
1 large banana	20 ml (4 tsp) salt
100 g (4 oz) preserved	5 ml (1 tsp) ground ginger
ginger	2.5 ml (½ tsp) pepper
2 medium onions	300 ml (½ pint) vinegar
2 lemons	

MAKES 900 g (2 lb)

Peel and chop the lychees. Peel and slice the banana. Slice the preserved ginger. Skin and grate the onions. Peel and cut the lemons into small chunks.

Put all the ingredients into an aluminium preserving pan and simmer for about 1½ hours. Mash to a rough purée with a plastic-coated masher.

Cool, then pack the chutney into clean jars. Cover and seal.

BANANA AND LYCHEE CHUTNEY (above)

Apple, Banana and Apricot Chutney

A slight suggestion of curry gives this sweet fruit chutney bite and zest. It is delicious in cheese sandwiches, and a great favourite on a picnic with children, who always seem to love the banana flavour which comes through so strongly.

100 g (4 oz) dried apricots	5 ml (1 tsp) ground ginger
900 g (2 lb) cooking apples	25 g (1 oz) curry powder
6 bananas	225 g (8 oz) soft brown sugar
350 g (12 oz) onions	600 ml (1 pint) vinegar
50 g (2 oz) salt	
5 ml (1 tsp) ground cinnamon	MAKES 1.8 kg (4 lb)

Rinse the apricots, cover with water and soak overnight. Wash, peel, core and slice the apples. Drain and chop the apricots. Peel and slice the bananas and onions.

Put all the ingredients into an aluminium preserving pan. Bring to the boil and simmer very gently for 1–1½ hours, stirring frequently, until thick.

Cool, then pack the chutney into clean jars. Cover and seal.

Date and Plum Chutney

Rich and spicy, this chutney is deliciously different and takes its place with style on a cold buffet table. It goes particularly well with salamis and pâtés, so comes into its own in the summer months for salad meals.

1.4 kg (3 lb) plums	5 ml (1 tsp) ground ginger
350 g (12 oz) dates	2.5 ml (½ tsp) ground black pepper
3 small onions	
600 ml (1 pint) malt vinegar	5 ml (1 tsp) grated nutmeg
700 g (1½ lb) sugar	
15 ml (1 tbsp) salt	MAKES 2.7 kg (6 lb)

Wipe, halve and stone the plums. Stone and chop the dates. Skin and finely slice the onions.

Put the plums in an aluminium preserving pan with the vinegar, dates and onions. Simmer for 15–20 minutes until soft.

Stir in the sugar, salt and spices. Simmer until the mixture thickens, stirring frequently to prevent burning.

Cool, then pack the chutney into clean jars. Cover and seal.

Pickles and Relishes

THE addition of pickles and relishes to salad meals, to buffet parties, and even to the simplest of Ploughman's lunches provides a delicious finishing touch. Their sharp tastes, often strong ones, go beautifully with rich foods like curries, or with simple egg and cheese dishes for example. Unusual ingredients such as watermelon rind and green walnuts come into their own in this department, and when there is a glut of summer vegetables this is a marvellous way of dealing with them to enjoy later in the year.

SUITABLE FRUIT AND VEGETABLES

A wide variety of fruits, vegetables, herbs and spices are used in pickles and relishes, ranging from cauliflower, shallots, kidney beans, apples, onions, artichokes and beetroot, to lemons, melons, peaches and pears. Gherkins and red cabbage are delicious pickled, as are mushrooms, along with less usual ingredients like walnuts, nasturtium seeds and watermelon rind. The art of making good pickles is to establish the right balance between sourness, saltiness and sweetness: you can make either of these three qualities predominate by adjusting the quantities of vinegar, salt and sugar.

BRINING TECHNIQUES

Brine is a solution of salt and water that is usually measured by percentage. A 10% brine is normally used when making vegetable pickles and relishes, and this requires 100 g (4 oz) salt to every 1.1 litres (2 pints) water. When vinegar is used in the preserving process, the percentage can be lowered to 5%, that is 50 g (2 oz) salt to every 1.1 litres (2 pints) water.

The vegetables are soaked in the brine with the vinegar and other ingredients before the preserving process begins. Sometimes alum is added at the end to keep the texture of the vegetables crisp.

A typical method for brining and pickling is to cut the vegetables into suitable sizes and cover with a 5% brine for 24 hours, keeping them weighted down with a plate to cover them completely. Drain them, rinse thoroughly with cold water and cover with spiced vinegar (see page 86). Keep for at least 2 months before using.

Whereas crisp pickles such as onions and red cabbage are best covered with cold vinegar; plums, damsons and walnuts are better covered with boiling or very hot vinegar, which is cooled before covering and sealing.

SPICES AND HERBS

Spices add zest and flavour to pickles and relishes and also have the added advantage that they are preservatives in their own right. The best ones to use are cloves, cinnamon, pepper, allspice, mace, nutmeg and ginger. Ground turmeric is sometimes added for its golden colour. Herbs are a traditional addition to many relishes and pickles, notably rue, fennel, sage, coriander and garlic and, most famous of all, dill.

Spiced Pickling Vinegar

**15 g (½ oz) each whole
cloves, allspice berries,
root ginger, cinnamon
sticks, whole
peppercorns
1.1 litres (2 pints) vinegar**

Steep the spices in the vinegar in a large bottle, without heating, for 1–2 months, shaking occasionally. Strain the vinegar and re-bottle. Keep covered, preferably with a cork.

For a quicker method, warm the vinegar in an aluminium preserving pan. Add the spices, cover and infuse over a low heat for 2 hours. Leave to cool. When cold, strain the vinegar into bottles.

◆ VINEGAR ◆

When making pickles and relishes, use the best quality vinegar possible, and check that it has an acetic acid content of at least 5%. Cheap vinegar is a false economy since the preserves will not keep so well. White vinegar shows off the colour and texture of a pickle better than a dark one, but for most domestic purposes malt vinegar gives perfectly satisfactory results.

◆ STORING ◆

Pickles and relishes are best stored in glass jars with plastic screw-tops. Do not use metal ones as these will be corroded by both the vinegar and the salt.

It is vital to keep the air out of jars of pickles and relishes since it causes discoloration, encourages moulds and degrades the vinegar by facilitating the invasion of bacteria. So fill the jars to their brim and cover carefully, making sure that there are no air bubbles. Pickles must be kept well below the surface of the vinegar or brine or mixture of the two. You can put a layer of oil over the top to seal it – mustard oil is the best one to use for this since it has preservative properties.

Where the vinegar solution is fairly dilute, the pickle will not keep for all that long because of the level of acidity. You can, however, skim off any scum as it forms and still eat the contents – it is natural and harmless, but do finish the pickles as quickly as possible once this starts to happen.

Times of storage vary considerably with different pickles and relishes: some are ready quickly, whereas others may need six months or more to mature.

◆ SERVING IDEAS ◆

Pickles and relishes are a marvellous and colourful contribution to a salad table – when it is laid out, a buffet looks quite sumptuous with a variety of home-made pickles dotted amongst the dishes. They are especially delicious with cheeses, with potted meats and in sandwiches. Pickles and relishes can be mixed into cottage cheese to sharpen it up, and are also excellent with freshly boiled ham.

PICKLED MUSHROOMS (page 88)

Sweet Watermelon Rind Pickle

Whoever had the bizarre idea of pickling watermelon rind was actually rather inspired: on the face of it, it seems unlikely to be delicious, yet cooked in a spiced syrup the peel turns translucent and crunchy, and is a superb addition to a cold buffet table.

1.8 kg (4 lb) watermelon rind	600 ml (1 pint) white vinegar
100 g (4 oz) salt	600 ml (1 pint) water
1.1 litres (2 pints) cold water	20 ml (4 tsp) whole cloves
900 g (2 lb) sugar	2×7.5 cm (3 inch) sticks cinnamon

MAKES 1.8 kg (4 lb)

Peel the dark skin off the rind and scrape off any traces of the pink fruit. Cut the rind into 1 cm (½ inch) cubes. Dissolve the salt in the cold water, add the rind cubes and steep for 6 hours.

Drain and rinse thoroughly. Put the rind into a saucepan and cover with fresh water. Simmer for 10 minutes until tender but not too soft. Drain.

Combine the sugar, vinegar and 600 ml (1 pint) water in an aluminium preserving pan. Tie the cloves and cinnamon in a muslin bag and add to the pan. Bring to the boil and simmer for 10 minutes. Pour the spiced vinegar over the rind cubes. Leave to stand overnight with the bag still in the mixture.

Bring to the boil again and simmer for 10 minutes until the rind is transparent. Remove the bag.

Transfer the rinds with a slotted spoon into warm, clean jars. Pour over the hot syrup. Cover and seal. Store for three weeks before using.

Pickled Mushrooms

This light and delicate method of pickling mushrooms retains their flavour and texture. They make a lovely cold side dish to go with other salads, and provide a delightful contribution to a picnic basket.

225 g (8 oz) small button mushrooms	300 ml (½ pint) wine vinegar
1 large onion	12 peppercorns
2 garlic cloves	3 bay leaves
600 ml (1 pint) water	sprig of rosemary
10 ml (2 tsp) salt	sprig of thyme

MAKES 450 g (1 lb)

Wipe the mushrooms clean. Skin and slice the onion. Bruise the garlic.

Put the mushrooms into a saucepan with the water and salt. Bring to the boil, then remove from the heat and leave to stand for 5 minutes. Drain and dry the mushrooms with a clean tea-towel.

Put the vinegar into an aluminium preserving pan with the spices, herbs, onion and garlic. Simmer for 15 minutes. Cool and strain.

Place the mushrooms in a clean jar and pour over the spiced vinegar. Cover and seal. Store for two to three weeks before using.

Sweetcorn Relish

When the sweetcorn crop is particularly plentiful, I love to make this relish. It is one of the most tempting both to look at and to taste. Sweetcorn relish is quite crunchy and slightly spicy, and one of the most popular all-rounders with family and friends alike.

6 corn cobs	10 ml (2 tsp) flour
½ white cabbage	10 ml (2 tsp) dry mustard
2 large onions	2.5 ml (½ tsp) turmeric
2 small red peppers	175 g (6 oz) brown sugar
10 ml (2 tsp) salt	600 ml (1 pint) vinegar

MAKES 1.8 kg (4 lb)

Put the corn cobs in a saucepan of boiling water and simmer for 3 minutes. Cool slightly then strip the corn kernels from the cobs.

Wash and mince the cabbage, onions and peppers in a food processor or mincer. Put into an aluminium preserving pan with the corn.

Mix the salt, flour, mustard, turmeric and sugar together thoroughly. Gradually stir in the vinegar, blending well. Add to the vegetables and simmer for 30 minutes.

Pack the relish into warm, clean jars. Cover and seal.

Cucumber Relish

The translucency of cucumber, slightly sweetened and spiced, looks beautiful in this pale green relish. In my house, this disappears rapidly during the summer months – it is an indispensible part of light salady meals and is delicious with cheeses.

2 cucumbers	450 g (1 lb) brown sugar
1.4 kg (3 lb) green tomatoes	450 g (1 lb) white sugar
	30 ml (2 tbsp) flour
1 green pepper	30 ml (2 tbsp) curry powder
1 red pepper	
8 onions	15 ml (1 tbsp) dry mustard
15 ml (1 tbsp) salt	
1.1 litres (2 pints) white vinegar	MAKES 3.6 kg (8 lb)

Wash and finely mince all the vegetables using a food processor or mincer. Put into a bowl and sprinkle with the salt. Cover and leave to stand overnight. Strain off the liquid.

Put the minced vegetables into an aluminium preserving pan with the vinegar and sugar. Bring to the boil and simmer for 1 hour.

Blend the flour, curry powder and mustard with a little vinegar to make a creamy paste and stir into the pan. Simmer for a further 30 minutes.

Pack the relish into warm, clean jars. Cover and seal.

Malay Vegetable Pickle

Crunchy and spicy, this uniquely Indonesian pickle is full of flavour and makes a kind of salad dish in its own right, highlighting other dishes of all kinds. I was introduced to it by an Indian friend of mine and now I wonder how I ever got along without it!

1 cucumber	225 g (8 oz) toasted
3 large carrots	sesame seeds
225 g (8 oz) cauliflower	10 ml (2 tsp) turmeric
4 green chillies	15 ml (1 tbsp) chilli
350 g (12 oz) dry-roasted	powder
peanuts	150 ml (¼ pint) vegetable
6 garlic cloves	oil
600 ml (1 pint) spiced	salt
vinegar (see page 86)	
225 g (8 oz) demerara	MAKES 2.3 kg (5 lb)
sugar	

Wash and cut the cucumber into 5 mm (¼ inch) slices. Wash, scrape and cut the carrots into 5 mm (¼ inch) slices. Wash and cut the cauliflower into florets. Wash and seed the chillies, then cut lengthwise. Coarsely grind the peanuts. Crush the garlic.

Bring the vinegar to the boil in an aluminium preserving pan. Add the vegetables, one type at a time in a large sieve, and scald by dunking them into the vinegar. Shake off as much of the vinegar as possible.

In a large bowl, mix the vegetables together with the sugar, peanuts and sesame seeds. Mix the turmeric and chilli powder to a paste with a little water.

Heat the oil in a pan and fry the garlic very gently for 1–2 minutes. Add the spice paste and salt to taste. Leave to cool. Stir the garlic mixture into the vegetables.

Pack the pickle into large, clean jars. This pickle will keep for several months if stored in a cool place.

Pickled Green Walnuts

An utterly English invention, this unlikely idea has been used by the country housewife for centuries. Nothing is better in its way than a lunch of bread, cheese and pickled walnuts.

700 g (1½ lb) green	6 cloves
walnuts	12 peppercorns
1.7 litres (3 pints) strong	1.7 litres (3 pints) spiced
brine (see page 85)	vinegar (see page 86)
4 large garlic cloves	
	MAKES 1.4 kg (3 lb)

Put the green walnuts into a large bowl. Pour over the brine and leave to soak for a week until they turn black. Put them into a colander and rinse thoroughly in hot water until the salt is washed off.

Prick the walnuts with a fork in order to let the spices permeate. Pack them into clean jars with the garlic, cloves and peppercorns amongst them.

Bring the spiced vinegar to the boil. Pour the hot vinegar over the walnuts. Leave to stand overnight.

Drain off the vinegar, reheat to boiling again and pour over the walnuts once more. Cover and seal.

MALAY VEGETABLE PICKLE (above)

Summer Relish

Delightfully easy to make, this is one way of converting a glut of summer vegetables so that you can enjoy them in later months. It looks gorgeous too – full of the colours of summer.

2 large carrots	150 ml (¼ pint) olive oil
1 green pepper	15 ml (1 tbsp) brown
12 green beans	sugar
1 courgette	30 ml (2 tbsp) chopped
12 green olives	fresh oregano
12 cherry tomatoes	75 ml (5 tbsp) water
450 g (1 lb) cauliflower	salt and pepper
florets	
300 ml (½ pint) wine	MAKES 1.8 kg (4 lb)
vinegar	

Wash, scrape and cut the carrots into julienne strips. Wash, deseed and cut the pepper into small cubes. Trim the green beans and cut into 2.5 cm (1 inch) lengths. Wash, trim and cut the courgette into julienne strips. Halve and stone the olives. Wash and quarter the cherry tomatoes.

Combine all the ingredients in an aluminium preserving pan and add salt and pepper to taste. Bring to the boil and simmer, stirring constantly, for 5 minutes.

Cool and leave to marinate for 24 hours.

Pack the relish into clean jars. Cover and seal.

Sour Chinese Cabbage Relish

This is taken from a traditional Korean recipe, where it is known as 'kimchee'. It is a kind of non-preserved chutney, one which keeps for a relatively short time but which is so different and unusual that I love to produce it to ring the changes.

700 g (1½ lb) Chinese	450 g (1 lb) salt
cabbage	30 ml (2 tbsp) ground
4 garlic cloves	ginger
6 spring onions	1 red chilli
1.4 litres (2½ pints) water	5 ml (1 tsp) sugar
	MAKES 1.8 kg (4 lb)

Wash and coarsely shred the Chinese cabbage leaves. Skin and chop the garlic. Wash, trim and finely slice the spring onions. Mix the water with the salt in a bowl. Add the cabbage and leave to soak for 12 hours, turning occasionally.

Mix the ginger, garlic, spring onion, chilli and sugar in a large bowl. Drain the cabbage, reserving the liquid, and combine with the mixture in the bowl.

Put the cabbage mixture into a large storage jar and cover with the salt water. Cover with a cloth and leave for about a week to ferment – it will be ready when it turns slightly sour.

Pack the relish into clean jars. Cover and seal. Store in a cool place for not longer than three weeks.

Red Pepper Relish

A lovely, piquant, strong relish that is only needed in quite small quantities – a little goes a long way. It is absolutely superb to accompany a simple meal of an omelette, a salad and some fresh bread.

900 g (2 lb) red peppers	1.4 kg (3 lb) white sugar
50 g (2 oz) mustard seeds	1.7 litres (3 pints) vinegar

MAKES 1.8 kg (4 lb)

Wash and remove the seeds from the peppers. Cut the flesh into fairly fine strips. Soak the mustard seeds in hot water for 2–3 hours. Strain.

Put all the ingredients into an aluminium preserving pan. Bring slowly to the boil, stirring until the sugar has dissolved. Boil rapidly for 15–20 minutes, stirring frequently, until the liquid begins to thicken.

Pack the relish into warm, clean jars. Cover and seal.

Green Coriander Relish

A typically Indian relish, this has a short storage life but is so delicious that I cannot resist making it when green coriander is plentiful. The coconut milk provides a lovely smoothness, and the balance of the garlic and spices with the coriander makes a very special condiment for a spicy eastern meal.

15 ml (1 tbsp) desiccated coconut	3 small green chillies
300 ml (½ pint) boiling water	juice of 2 limes
2 bunches fresh coriander	2.5 ml (½ tsp) salt
2 garlic cloves	5 ml (1 tsp) soft brown sugar
1 cm (½ inch) fresh root ginger	5 ml (1 tsp) ground cumin

MAKES 900 g (2 lb)

Allow the coconut to steep in the boiling water for 30 minutes. Wash and chop the coriander. Crush the garlic. Peel and grate the ginger. Wash and chop the chillies. Blend the coconut mixture in a food processor or blender, then strain through a sieve.

Combine all the ingredients with the coconut milk and blend in a food processor, adding a very little water if necessary to obtain a smooth paste.

Pack the relish into clean jars. Cover and seal. Store in the refrigerator for up to three weeks.

Tomato Relish

A lovely sharp, fresh relish with a light spiciness to it. With its contrasting textures of tomatoes, cucumber and red pepper, this mixture is delicious with cold meats like roast lamb, and gorgeous with a Ploughman's lunch.

1.5 kg (3 lb) tomatoes
500 g (1 lb) cucumber or
  marrow
50 g (2 oz) salt
2 garlic cloves
1 large red pepper
450 ml (¾ pint) white
  vinegar

15 ml (1 tbsp) dry
  mustard
2.5 ml (½ tsp) ground
  allspice
2.5 ml (½ tsp) mustard
  seeds

MAKES ABOUT 1.5 kg (3 lb)

Skin and slice the tomatoes. Peel, seed and roughly chop the cucumber or marrow. Layer the tomatoes and cucumber or marrow in a bowl, sprinkling each layer with salt. Cover and leave to stand overnight.

Strain off the liquid and rinse well and place in a large saucepan. Skin and finely chop the garlic. Wash, seed and roughly chop the pepper and add these to the pan. Blend the vinegar with the dry ingredients, stir into the pan and bring slowly to the boil. Simmer gently for about 1 hour, stirring occasionally, until the mixture is soft. Spoon the relish into warm, clean jars and cover. Seal immediately. Store for 3–4 months before use.

Sweet-Sour Apricots

I love fresh apricots – one of the most delicate and beautiful of our summer fruits, I always think. Preserved in this way, with a tang and spiciness added to their natural fruitiness, they also look glorious nestling in their glistening syrup.

375 ml (12 fl oz) wine
  vinegar
275 g (9 oz) granulated
  sugar

500 g (1 lb) apricots
1 small cinnamon stick

Pour the vinegar into a saucepan, add the sugar and heat gently, stirring, until the sugar has dissolved, then bring to the boil. Peel the apricots. Put the apricots into a warm, clean jar, packing as lightly as possible, add the cinnamon stick and slowly pour in the hot vinegar syrup. Cover immediately with an airtight and vinegar-proof top.

Note: These pickled apricots are best left for a month before using. Serve with pork, ham or chicken.

Index